Sun-
bonnet
Sisters

Leonard J. Arrington • Susan Arrington Madsen

Sun-
bonnet
Sisters

True Stories of Mormon Women and Frontier Life

Bookcraft

Salt Lake City, Utah

Library of Congress Catalog Card Number: 84-70067
ISBN 0-88494-520-0

First Printing, 1984

#10528954

Lithographed in the United States of America
PUBLISHERS PRESS
Salt Lake City, Utah

To our mothers

Edna and Grace Arrington

Contents

Part Four: Second-Generation Achievers

Preface

The official histories of the Latter-day Saints tend to concentrate, quite understandably, on the prophets and their associates in establishing the structure of the Church and supervising the work of the leaders. Biographies have been written principally about priesthood leaders—Apostles, seventies, stake presidents, and bishops. We are delighted to observe that more attention is now being given to writing about Latter-day Saint women—about their special and abundant contributions to the building of the kingdom.

We have wanted to contribute to that trend of increased attention by relating the lives of some of the earlier Latter-day Saint women. While the accounts cover their entire lives, in this preface and in the introduction we call attention more especially to their earlier years. If the child is father of the man, as Wordsworth asserted, surely the girl is mother of the woman. We can learn much about pioneering by studying the lives of the girls who went through the experience.

With the help of Davis Bitton's *Guide to Mormon Diaries and Autobiographies,* we have located approximately two hundred diaries and reminiscences that treat in some detail women's experiences as children in the nineteenth century. Some of these have been published privately by families or by the Daughters of the Utah Pioneers. But the majority are in manuscript form in the holdings of the LDS Church Archives in Salt Lake City and the Utah State Historical Society, and in the special collections of Brigham Young University, Utah State University, and the University of Utah. From the material available, we have selected the seventeen ''lives'' that are presented here. These seventeen, we feel, not only are intrinsically interesting, but also help to illustrate little-known facts of Latter-day Saint history.

On April 6, 1830, when The Church of Jesus Christ of Latter-day Saints was founded, among those almost certainly present at the organizational meeting were seven teenage girls. One of these was Elizabeth Ann Whitmer, age fifteen, at whose parents' home the meeting was held. Two others were Catherine and Lucy Smith, ages seventeen and nine, sisters of the Prophet Joseph Smith, who convened the meeting. Another set of sisters present was Caroline and Electa Rockwell, ages thirteen and eleven, whose mother and brother Porter were also present and among the first baptized into the new faith. Sarah or Sally Heller, age nineteen, who helped with the work of the Whitmer household until her marriage shortly thereafter, was also there, and probably helped with the refreshments after the meeting was concluded. Finally, Polly Knight, also nineteen, daughter of Joseph Knight, one of the very first converts to the Church, was probably there with other residents of Colesville, New York, who had come as believers. Other girls may have been there whose presence the documents do not declare. It must have been an exciting moment for all to remember, and to recount to their husbands, children, and grandchildren in the years that followed.

Ever since that momentous first meeting of the Restored Church, girls have played important roles in building the kingdom: in supporting their mothers and fathers, in helping their sisters and brothers, in assisting the ward bishops and Relief Society presidents, and in serving their communities as teachers, skilled workers, and homemakers. Eventually, most of them have married, had children, maintained Latter-day Saint homes, and functioned in a variety of capacities in Church and community activities: in the Primary Association, Young Women's Mutual Improvement Association, Sunday School, Women's Relief Society, and in various civic bodies and cultural groups. Some have been elected to public office.

Some of the "girls" described in this book were born into the Church; others joined at various stages of their childhood or adolescence. Some were born in Utah or an adjacent state; others were born in the East, South, Midwest, or in Europe or Canada. Some were reared in families with wealth or position; others were very poor. Some of them achieved widespread recognition, even while young; others became "simple housewives." Each of the seventeen married and had children, one of them giving birth to sixteen! All of them, the rich and the poor, the well known and the not so well known, were faithful Latter-day Saints according to their own lights. All had life stories that are well worth telling.

In the lives of these girls and young women we get a picture of the tempestuous nature of early Church history, the epoch-making trek to the Salt Lake Valley, the planned colonizing of settlements, and the building of cities. We also obtain an understanding of the work people did, the food they ate, the clothing they wore, the homes they lived in, the games they played, and the schooling they received. Finally, we learn what it meant to be a girl in a settlement of Zion, and the conditions under which the young women were married and transformed into "mothers in Israel."

For help in preparing this book we are grateful to Maureen Ursenbach Beecher, Carol Cornwall Madsen, Lavina Fielding Anderson, Jill Mulvay Derr, and Ida M. Smith. We also appreciate the help of Davis Bitton, Donald Schmidt, Richard Jensen, Kathleen Hardy Anderson, and Jeff Simmonds. We express special gratitude to our respective spouses, Harriet Ann Arrington and Dean Madsen, for their support and encouragement. And we hope our children, especially our daughters and granddaughters, will like this book.

LEONARD J. ARRINGTON

SUSAN ARRINGTON MADSEN

Introduction

In the summer of 1885, almost one hundred years ago, Colenda Chrilla Rogers was living with her family in Pleasant Grove, Utah—the strawberry capital of pioneer Mormondom. During that summer Colenda sewed a dress for her mother, wrote letters for her Aunt Lizzie, helped with the farm work, did the family washing, walked to Provo to see a circus, went regularly to Sunday School, picked wild berries, cut and dried apples and peaches, went on outings with her chums, and in general helped out with the work of home and farm, village and church.

We know about Colenda's work and fun that summer because she kept a diary. Nor was it uncommon for pioneer girls to keep diaries. A number of these are in the LDS Church Archives in Salt Lake City, in university libraries, and in the possession of family descendants. What was it like to grow up as a girl in pioneer Utah? What did pioneer girls do? How did they react? What were they like?

The first striking fact is that many of our pioneer girls were born abroad, or were born of parents who emigrated from other countries when the girls were small children. In 1870, approximately half the white (i.e., non-Indian) adults in Utah were foreign-born. In 1890, a year for which we have more detailed demographic data, Utah's white population, if we exclude those under ten years of age, consisted of 30 percent native Americans with native parents, 35 percent native with foreign parentage, and 34 percent foreign-born. In other words, approximately 70 percent of Utah's white residents had foreign-born parents. A little over half of these foreign-born in Utah's first thirty years were born in the British Isles, and a little less than half in Scandinavia, principally Denmark. Obviously, there was a problem of adjustment to Utah's semiarid land, but there must have been an even more important problem of adjustment between the various nationalities—their language, culture, and way of life.

A second striking fact is that a surprisingly large number of girls suffered because of the early death of one or both parents. Only a small percentage of households still had both parents alive by the time the last child had left the nest. A mother might die in childbirth, from tuberculosis (which the pioneers called "consumption''), or from one of the other frequent diseases—cholera, pneumonia, measles, or smallpox. The father might die of an accident, exposure, or, like his wife, of one of the common diseases of the period. The impact on the children is clear. They were brought up by a single parent, or with a second father or mother, or by an uncle or aunt, or by foster parents. These were not always happy arrangements. In many instances it meant poverty, lack of schooling, and going to work at an early age.

For a similar reason, many of the girls suffered through the deaths of little brothers or sisters or neighborhood playmates. A heavy proportion of all the babies died before they were one year of age, and of those who survived infancy, about one-fourth died before they reached sixteen. So death was an ever-present reality. The girls themselves—that is, those who lived—almost inevitably went through long sieges of illness: smallpox, typhoid fever, scarlet fever, diphtheria (which the pioneers called "putrid sore throat"), and, of course, mumps, whooping cough, and measles. It was not only the diseases that sapped their strength and energy, but the remedies—heavy doses of emetics, laxatives, mustard plasters, poultices, and the green flannel, foul-smelling asafetida bags worn around their necks each winter "to keep the germs away."

A third surprising fact is the frequency with which most pioneer families moved. Nearly every family moved their place of residence every two or three years. Lucy White's parents, for example, had lived in nine different locations by the time she was seventeen. One of these was a dugout in Salina, Sevier County. Rachel Pyne, who came to Utah with her parents from England when she was four, lived in eight different homes by the time she was eight. "We moved so often," Melinda Bean said, "that after living in one place for several weeks the chickens would come in and lie down on the floor with their legs together ready to be tied for the next move."

Partly because of the moving, partly because of poverty, most girls received very little education. Wards and settlements usually held school for three months each winter. That is, there was school *provided* someone was available and willing to teach, *provided* the heads of households were willing and able to support the teacher with vegetables and other produce, and *provided* there was no emergency facing the settlement such as danger from hostile Indians, the necessity of repairing a dam, or an epidemic of smallpox, whooping cough, measles, diphtheria, or some other contagious disease. Most girls did well to learn to read, write, and do simple arithmetic. Sometimes they learned this in Sunday School, since day school was so uncertain and infrequent.

Recognizing their inadequacy, some of the girls went to heroic lengths to teach themselves. Mathilde Nielsen, born in Copenhagen, was brought to the United States when she was six, and her family settled in a Scandinavian village in Morgan County called Milton. The family was very poor. Mathilde had to milk ten cows and do the housework; card, spin, weave, and sew; and help tend her little brothers and sisters. Her mother died when she was twelve; Mathilde had to "get out and rustle," as she expressed it. By the time she was sixteen, she was working in a household in Ogden, making $3 per week. While there, she received a letter from her brother Waldemer, asking her to write home. But she had never written a letter! Let her tell the story:

> I will never forget my first letter that I ever tried to write. My brother insisted I write when he knew I had never had a pencil in my hand. But I was game. I got a book with the letters in and a lead pencil and paper, and started to write. It didn't look so bad while I was writing, but when I got it finished I couldn't read one word. I rolled it in a little ball and started to cry and was going to put it in the stove. I changed my mind. Instead, I sat down, smoothed it out, and sent it. I thought he would never ask me to write again. Just as quick as my brother could answer, a letter came back. He said he could read every word. If he hadn't answered my questions I would have thought he was fibbing. He begged me to write again. I did and kept on writing until it looked pretty fair.

Mathilde continued to write the rest of her life, and because of that her grandchildren and great-grandchildren are able to know about her fascinating life. Her legacy was a marvelous, if brief, personal history.

What did these pioneer girls do? Mostly, it would seem, they worked. They helped their mothers; they helped their fathers; they helped their grandparents, if one or more was near; they helped their neighbors; they helped their brothers and sisters. The specific tasks of the girl, in most instances, were to help with the housework and gardenwork; glean the fields; gather the eggs, fruit, and vegetables; make butter, cheese, and soap; help make all the clothing, including hats, worn by the family; help feed the pigs, chickens, horses, and cattle, and sometimes herd them; trim the lamp wicks and clean the chimneys; and do all kinds of errands. The hours of work were "all of them," and the tasks were "whatever you can do." Yet even in their poverty and economizing there could be the saving grace of humor. Once a family in southern Utah was at supper, when the little brother called out, "Ma, Jake's wasty! He picked a fly out of the 'lasses and never licked its legs off." "Wasty Jake Beecham" was a byword around town for years.

Sarah Ann Murdock, the eldest child of a large family, had gone with her parents in the 1850s to Carson Valley, Nevada, where her father was appointed to take care of the Church cattle and make butter and cheese for the tithing office. When they were returning to Utah across the Nevada deserts, her mother began her labor for the next child. The wagon was halted in the shelter of a large rock. Since it reminded him of Mount Sinai, the father, after delivering the baby girl, blessed her and named her Rocksinai.

The family eventually moved to Heber Valley. Whenever one of their friends or neighbors got her rolls of wool prepared, she would invite other women and girls to bring their spinning wheels and help get the rolls spun into yarn.

"We would go early in the morning and spin all day, stopping only to eat dinner prepared by the hostess. One day I spun ten skeins, which ordinarily would have taken two or three days. . . . Four skeins was supposed to be a good day's work."

When the local congregation needed rags to make a rug for the meetinghouse, Bessie Brown and Lila Eliason suggested that they hold a rag dance. Everyone had to bring some rags to gain admittance into the dance. The day after the dance, the young ladies and the Relief Society women made the carpet.

Nancy Greene's mother settled in Escalante, in what was called Potato Valley, and Nancy, the eldest daughter in a family of six, had a lot of cows to milk. "Among my mother's cows," she wrote, "was one old cow which would not let a man come near her. If for any reason one of the men had to handle her, he would have to put on a woman's dress, apron, and sunbonnet. We children thought this very funny."

Carrie Laub, in Hebron, remembered when she and her mother went out to the watermelon patch and enjoyed a watermelon. Her father ate with them and then went to work, but her mother stayed with her and continued eating. In a few minutes her father came back and said, "You still eating?" and the mother replied, "I am going to eat enough so in the winter when they are all gone, I won't wish I had eaten some more when I had a chance."

Frances Richards, whose parents lived in Union Fort, Salt Lake County, in the 1860s, lived on a family farm. She learned to milk at five, and helped put up the hay, raking it with hand rakes and piling it with hand forks. In the summer and fall she and her friends had apple-cutting bees and peach-cutting bees. "These were considered as recreation," she wrote. "We would frequently cut as many as 25 bushels in one evening." The next day these were spread on the housetops and on scaffolds to dry.

About the age of fourteen, many of the girls had to work outside the home to bring in income. A girl usually began working for neighbors, then at a better spot out of town, and eventually, in the course of her work, she would meet the man who would become her husband. Mathilde Nielsen had to work away from home as early as twelve years of age. She milked ten cows and did the housework, earning 50 cents per week. Her remark about this to her children was: "I had to go barefooted to do it all. When a cow stepped on your bare feet it sure did hurt." By the time she was fifteen, Mathilde was taking care of new mothers and their babies. When she was seventeen she went to Ogden to work for an LDS family for two years at $3 per week, and was able to buy many of the things her family needed.

Mary Hobson was born in 1852 in Farmington, Utah, the eighth in a family of nine children. She later kept house for her older brother Alma, who had a store in Richmond, Utah. The first telegraph operator there, he taught Mary, age fifteen, telegraphy and sent her to a special school for this in Logan. As his assistant she was the first woman telegrapher in Richmond. Then Alma moved to Franklin, the oldest town in Idaho, where he kept a store, post office, and telegraph office. Mary helped him, thus becoming the first woman telegrapher in Idaho. When Alma moved back to Richmond, Mary stayed in Franklin and managed the store, post office, and telegraph office for several years.

The kinds of tasks given to the girls and young women were calculated to give them not only a sense of responsibility but also a feeling of self-confidence. Among the Saints no distinction was made between the mistress of a house and a servant girl working for her. The girl ate with the family, prayed with them, played with them. Her assigned work unquestionably gave her a feeling of accomplishment. And much of the work was not stereotyped "woman's work." Girls were asked to do what had to be done— whatever they were resourceful and courageous and skilled enough to do. Violet Lunt Urie wrote that when she was little, she accompanied a relative to a mountain near Cedar City, taking her doll along with her. "When I arrived at the mountain cabin," she wrote, "I found a place to put my doll in the cupboard. Just then someone called to tell me to tend the kids. From then on I found there were always too many kids for me to have time for dolls." Violet said that when she was nine, she and an eleven-year-old boy were given the task of driving thirty-five pigs from Jones Hollow (on the mountain) to Cedar City. When she was fourteen, she was assigned to drive the family calves from the mountain to town. Although she was supposed to help her married sister with the housework, she had to get up early to drive animals, shuck corn, and do other farm work before she was "released" to do housework. But this wasn't all drudgery: "There were jolly times around the campfire, playing hide and seek, or run-sheep-run by the light of the moon after the chores were done."

An inevitable female task in almost every household in which the girls grew up was making cloth and clothing. As early as age five or six the girls were knitting with two needles, and within a year they were knitting pairs of stockings with long legs and double heels from yarn which their mother or older sisters had carded, spun, and dyed. By the time they were twelve they had learned to spin. Sarah Ann Owen, in Cache Valley, remembers spending long hours spinning on a machine that required the spinner to stand. "We found," she wrote, "that by removing our shoes and standing in water that we poured on the barn floor, we could relieve the aching of our feet while standing all day spinning." Most of the girls learned to embroider, crochet, and tat when they were thirteen or fourteen. Some of them, at the same age, also learned to weave. Not all households had looms, of course, but often there was one or more in every neighborhood.

The making of cloth and clothing in the home was partly a necessity, considering their poverty and their distance from markets with machine-made products. Textile material was scarce in the 1850s and '60s, and in some areas also in the 1870s and '80s. One girl reported that she saw a woman rip up an old dress to make over for one of her children. "She picked out the stitches one by one," the girl reported, "and saved the thread to restitch it with."

Many households raised their own sheep, clipped the wool, prepared it for spinning, spun it, and then took it to a neighbor with a loom to weave it into linsey. The linsey was then cut and made into skirts, blouses, shirts, dresses, and men's suits. Mary Julia Johnson stated that a young man who was to leave for a mission in one week had no suit to wear. When the women of the ward heard this, they went to work. The result was that "one Sunday the wool was on the sheep's back, but by the next Sunday it had been clipped, cleansed, carded, spun, woven, and made into a splended suit and was on the back of the missionary as he delivered his farewell address in our little church house."

Even the herding of the sheep and the clipping of the wool was often done by the girls, particularly when they had no brothers or when their brothers had other work to do. Many girls had some herding experience, and a few did all the herding. Minerva Stone herded her father's little band of fifteen or twenty sheep on the bench east of Ogden. Her work included feeding and raising the lambs whose mothers had disowned them. In getting the sheep back to her home each evening, she often followed paths lined with cockleburs. She was barefooted.

"I would hesitate," she wrote, "and wonder whether it be the least painful to run over the burrs or to walk slowly. Running would be more acute, but sooner ended, while walking slowly would prolong my misery. However my supply of shoe leather [the soles of her naked feet] was inexhaustible. As soon as one thickness would wear off, another would grow in its place."

Remembering that there were no such things as coats in many pioneer homes, and no central heating, it is easy to understand why the girls wore so many layers of underclothing. Mamie Woolley, who lived most of her years in St. George and Kanab—not exactly a cold country—described the clothing girls wore in the 1880s and '90s.

> Our garments or unions reached from the neck to the ankle, with long sleeves to the wrist, and were made of heavy factory [cloth], which had to be bleached for weeks, by boiling and then spreading it on the

lucerne patch where it could get the direct rays of the sun, and it had to be wet every day during the process.

On top of the garment or union we wore a "chemise" which reached far below the knees, was made of bleach, or factory, and more or less elaborately trimmed with tucks and insertion to form a yoke, and narrow lace or embroidery was ruffled around the neck and arm-holes. . . .

We never wore less than two petticoats and often three or more. Mother never considered us well nor modestly dressed without a white flannel or linsey petticoat "next to us" (on top of all the other things mentioned) and then a red or gray flannel one over that in winter. In summer the extra one could be made of cotton, either bleach, all tucked and ruffled, or black satine [sateen], as we liked; but they must be made as full as they could possibly be gathered on to the waistband to conceal the outline of the figure and make them entirely shadowproof.

Over these underclothes they had tight-fitting basques or bodices, with stitched tapering folds or "darts" and "side bodies" to fit the bodice to the curves of the body, making at least ten seams in the waist, each one of which had to be "overcast" or sewed over the edge to prevent raveling and "boned" or strengthened with stays. Buttonholes were placed so close together down the front that the buttons usually touched, and sometimes overlapped each other. All of the sewing of these garments, it must be kept in mind, and also the boys' unions and shirts, was done by hand, by the mothers and the girls.

As for the skirts, they were three or four yards around the bottom, made either circular or with twelve to fifteen gores or sections, flared lengthwise, all lined throughout with skirt lining and interlined with crinoline to above the knees. The skirt, of course, reached to the ankle, and its heavy weight caused considerable friction on the girls' high-topped shoes. Together with the numerous petticoats, the heavy skirt always hung on the hips, never being suspended from the shoulders.

All of the clothing was made for growing girls and boys, and in the usual family had to last at least a year. So the clothes were always made a little large. In this way the children could grow into them, as it were. Girls sometimes complained that their party dresses, when first tried on, were "much too large," but the mothers helped by putting in tucks and temporary hems that would make them suitable for immediate wearing.

Despite the ration of one new dress or skirt per year for each girl, and one new suit for each male, there was always more work involved than they could do. A Cache Valley resident recalled that he did not remember ever seeing his mother or sisters in bed. ''They were up in the morning before any of us, and the last to bed.'' And this resident recalled that when his mother died, ''she did not look natural because she didn't have her knitting in her hands.''

Some households, of course, did not have enough girls to do all the spinning and sewing that was necessary for the members of the household, or perhaps the mother was dead, or perhaps she was ill for an extended period. In that event, the custom was to invite a neighbor girl to join the household. Some experienced girls who were fourteen, fifteen, or sixteen earned some income by spending time at neighboring households helping with the sewing tasks. When the spinning hours were over, they helped in the kitchen.

The customary picture of pioneer boys doing the outside work and girls performing the inside tasks is only partly correct. Girls, regularly in some families and occasionally in most, also worked in the fields, milked cows, pitched hay, and herded the livestock. It is not true that boys did the *hard* pioneering while girls led a more protected inside life. Girls shared in many of the work assignments traditionally thought to have been done only by boys, and girls shared the ''hardness'' of pioneering work along with the boys.

We must also remember that the girls participated in ward plays, ward choirs, ward dances, and ward outings; they were sometimes terrorized by hostile or supposedly hostile Indians, and sometimes by wild animals and reptiles and natural disasters; they were impressed with the nearness and reality of God and with the good example of most of their religious leaders; and they were full of spirit and courage. They contributed much to the building of the kingdom.

Given the conditions indicated, it would not be surprising if these young people developed into women of character and purpose who in their turn assumed the responsibilities of motherhood and family, Church callings, and community building. Our stories show this to have been the case. With pioneer resourcefulness, many who lacked formal education found some way to make up for that lack. Frequently, early poverty and the consequent compulsion to work hard at any early age brought experience and self-confidence that enabled them to make the most of their situation. Pioneer institutions like the Sunday School, the Young Ladies' Mutual Improvement Association, and the Relief Society encouraged and facilitated the development of talents and abilities. Writing their pioneer diaries and journals gave a further boost to their self-confidence and sense of perspective and helped them to mature gracefully. Building on the heritage such conditions produced, many of the second generation of Latter-day Saint women in particular were outstandingly successful in combining Church service, professional achievement, and family life.

The accounts in this book, carrying the stories from the early years to the end of mortal life, portray endurance, resilience, faith, a sense of responsibility, and a creative approach to life. As a reminder that we should all be awake to our opportunities and responsibilities, these lives are a splendid example and model for today's women, both younger and older, to build on.

Part One

In the Early Days of the Church

1

Mary Elizabeth Rollins Lightner
A Mormon Girl with Courage

In the early days of the Church, the first members were subjected to many trials and hardships. They had accepted a new faith, followed an unpopular prophet, and left their homes, whether in cities or country villages, to gather together to establish the kingdom of God. Though only a teenager in those difficult days, Mary Elizabeth Rollins was one of the most valiant and courageous of the early Saints.

Born in 1818 in Lima, Livingston County, in western New York State, Mary Elizabeth was ten years old when her father, John D. Rollins, drowned while sailing during a terrible storm on Lake Ontario. His wife, Keziah, was left with Mary and two other small children, James Henry and a six-month-old baby, Caroline.

Keziah took her little family across the border to Kirtland, Ohio, where they could live in a house owned by her brother-in-law, Algernon Sidney Gilbert. There, when Mary was twelve, she and her mother, uncle, and aunt were first introduced to the restored gospel. The first group of missionaries ever sent out by the Church went to Kirtland in October 1830. They took with them the newly printed Book of Mormon, which they testified had been found and translated by the latter-day prophet, Joseph Smith. Twelve-year-old Mary was impressed with the young missionaries—they were in their twenties, like most modern missionaries—and wrote: "They bore powerful testimony, by the Holy Spirit, of the truth of the great work they were engaged in; and which they were commissioned by the Father to present to all the world."

Mary's testimony of the truthfulness of their message was strengthened when she met and talked with Oliver Cowdery and David Whitmer, two of the Three Witnesses, who bore record that they had actually seen the gold plates from which the Book of Mormon was translated.

Mary and her mother were baptized in the fall of 1830, becoming two of the earliest converts to The Church of Jesus Christ of Latter-day Saints. After her baptism Mary was eager to read the Book of Mormon, but the few copies that had been printed were in the hands of missionaries and Church leaders. John Whitmer, another witness to the existence of the gold plates, left a single copy of the book with Isaac Morley, who was serving as president of the little branch of Saints in Kirtland. Mary wrote of her efforts to borrow the new volume of scriptures:

> I went to [Brother Morley's] house . . . and asked to see the Book. [He] put it in my hand. As I looked at it, I felt such a desire to read it, that I could not refrain from asking him to let me take it home and read it. . . . He said . . . he had hardly had time to read a chapter in it himself, and but few of the brethren had even seen it. But I pleaded so earnestly for it, he finally said, "Child, if you will bring this book home before breakfast tomorrow morning, you may take it."

Mary was overjoyed, and dashed home to show the "Golden Bible" to her aunt and uncle. "If any person in this world was ever perfectly happy in the possession of any coveted treasure I was," she said.

Mary was reprimanded for being so "presumptuous" as to ask for the book when so many others wanted to see it. But she retired to the family dinner table, where she read late into the night by candlelight. She made a point of memorizing the first verse before returning the book to Brother Morley early the next morning, proudly showing him how far she had read. Surprised, he remarked, "I don't believe you can tell me one word of it." Mary wrote:

> I then repeated the first verse, also the outlines of the history of Nephi. He gazed at me in surprise, and said, "Child, take this book home and finish it; I can wait."

Mary returned home, clinging tightly to the precious book she would now be able to finish reading. She was almost certainly the first resident of Kirtland to read the entire Book of Mormon.

Within a month, Mary's uncle's business partner, Newel K. Whitney, brought a guest to meet Mary and her family. Mary was not home, but was sent for with the message that the Prophet Joseph Smith was waiting to meet her. Joseph had been told of young Mary and her interest in reading the Book of Mormon. Mary wrote of the meeting:

> When he saw me he looked at me so earnestly, I felt almost afraid. After a moment or two he came and put his hands on my head and gave me a great blessing, the first I ever received, and made me a present of the book, and said he would give Brother Morley another. . . . We all felt that he was a man of God, for he spoke with power, and as one having authority.

During these months in Kirtland, Mary Elizabeth became acquainted not only with the Prophet but with nearly all the early members of the Church. She talked with all those who saw or handled the gold plates. She was even present at the very first meeting the Prophet conducted in Kirtland. In fact, she was probably responsible for it. The Smith family had just made the move from New York to Kirtland during the winter of 1830-1831. The day after they arrived in Kirtland, Mary suggested to her mother that they ought to go over to the Smiths to learn more about the plates and the translation which resulted in the Book of Mormon. Mary wrote that when they went in the house they found the entire Smith family, including Joseph Smith, Sr., Lucy Mack Smith, and all their children but the Prophet. There were also two or three others present, she said. Mary wrote:

> As we stood there talking to them, Joseph and Martin Harris came in. Said [Joseph], "There are enough here to hold a little meeting." Joseph looked around very solemnly. It was the first time some of them had ever seen him. They got a board and put it across two chairs to make seats. Martin Harris sat on a little box at Joseph's feet. They sang and prayed. Joseph got up and began to speak to us. As he began to speak very solemnly and very earnestly, all at once his countenance changed and he stood mute. [There seemed to be] a searchlight within him, over every part of his body. . . . I could not take my eyes off of him.

Mary then said there was a spiritual experience in which the little group were visited by an other-worldly presence. All of them were thrilled in their very being. Joseph then knelt down and prayed. "I never heard anything like it before or since," Mary wrote. "He talked to the Lord, and then gave us a sermon as though he was a direct representative from God."

The next year, in 1831, Mary moved to Independence, Missouri, with her mother, brother, and sister, accompanied by Church leaders W. W. Phelps and Bishop Edward Partridge. They were joined in Independence by several hundred other Saints and enjoyed "both spiritual and temporal prosperity."

Mary's "spiritual prosperity" soon manifested itself. Church leaders Oliver Cowdery, John Whitmer, and Thomas B. Marsh had come to Mary's uncle's home to discuss recent revelations Joseph Smith had received for the Church. The mood was reverent and humble, and the men soon began speaking in tongues. Mary, thirteen, was called up to interpret and she did so, "feeling the spirit of it in a moment."

Peace and prosperity did not last long for Mary and the other Saints in Missouri. Unfriendly mobs soon formed in an attempt to drive the believers from the state. "We were too much united to suit the inhabitants of Missouri," Mary wrote, "and they did not believe in our religion, or our way of doing business." The mobs set fire to haystacks, and fields of grain and destroyed homes, barns, businesses, and crops. Mary's home was stoned until all the windows were broken, and then the roof was torn off "amid fearful oaths and yells that were terrible to hear." She was not yet fourteen when she watched in horror as a family friend, Bishop Partridge, was tarred and feathered in the streets of Independence.

Several days later, Mary and her sister Caroline saw an angry mob enter the two-story Church printing office near their home. Brother W. W. Phelps and his family, who lived in the building, were driven out. Their belongings were tossed into the street, and the printing equipment was destroyed.

The mob soon emerged with a stack of paper on which had been printed the Book of Commandments (the first printing of what later came to be known as the Doctrine and Covenants). "Here are the Mormon Commandments," one of them shouted as he tossed them to the ground. Mary, standing nearby in the corner of the lot, was determined to save some of the copies. While the mob had their backs turned, Mary and Caroline dashed up, grabbed as many as they could carry, and hurried back behind the building. Some of the men turned around just in time to see the two girls and yelled at them to stop. Fearing for their lives, the girls ran through a gap in a wooden fence, raced into a cornfield, and hid on the ground, lying on top of the sheets of paper. The corn was five or six feet tall and the girls were well hidden. They lay very still for some time, listening to the mob as they searched the field for them. Several times they could see the men's feet as they walked among the cornstalks, but the girls were not discovered.

When it was safe to move, Mary and Caroline found Brother Phelps's wife and family hiding in a nearby barn. Sister Phelps took the sheets from the girls and later had them bound, giving each girl a copy. They prized these highly the rest of their lives. The copies Mary and Caroline saved are the only ones in existence today.

The persecutions soon became so severe that the Saints were again forced to flee, this time northward, across the Missouri River into sparsely settled country. When the group Mary's family was traveling with arrived on the banks of the river, they did not have enough money to cross the river on the ferry. Several of the brethren set out fishing poles, hoping to persuade the ferryman to accept the catch as payment in kind. The next morning they brought in the lines, finding three small fish and a catfish weighing fourteen pounds. Mary reported watching in amazement as a man opened the catfish to clean it and found three bright silver half dollars inside, just the amount needed to pay for having their party taken across the river. "This was considered a miracle," Mary wrote, "and caused great rejoicing among us."

Mary and her family settled in Clay County, Missouri. In an effort to become self-supporting, Mary, still only sixteen, began to teach spelling, reading, and writing to the children of the community. While teaching, she became acquainted with Adam Lightner of Liberty, Clay County, Missouri; they were married in 1835, when Mary was seventeen.

Troubles for the Saints in Missouri came to a crisis in 1838 when Governor Lilburn W. Boggs issued his infamous "Order of Extermination." "The Mormons," he declared, "must be treated as enemies and must be exterminated or driven from the state, if necessary, for the public good." General John B. Clark of the state militia was instructed, however, that before he carried out the order he was to make sure one nineteen-year-old Saint, Mary Rollins Lightner, and her immediate family were safely removed from danger.

Governor Boggs had become acquainted with Mary when, at the age of thirteen, she helped make some of the clothes he wore to his inauguration as lieutenant governor. Mary wrote:

> As I was considered a good seamstress, [Mr. Boggs] hired me to make his fine ruffled bosom shirts, also to assist his wife in her sewing. I worked for him for some weeks during that time. They tried to induce me to leave the [Latter-day Saints] Church and live with them; they would educate me and do for me as if I were their daughter . . . But their persuasions were of no avail with me.

Governor Boggs's offer to spare Mary from the violence that would soon threaten Far West, Missouri, led to a dramatic meeting between General Clark and this determined young woman. Mary asked the general if the other Mormon women and children would be allowed to leave with her. When the answer was no, she announced firmly, "If that is the case, I refuse to go, for where they die, I will die. I am a full blooded Mormon, and I am not ashamed to own it. I [will] suffer with the rest." At that moment, a gentleman who had been sitting nearby leaped to his feet and said, "Sister Lightner, God Almighty bless you. I thank God for one soul that is ready to die for her religion; not a hair of your head shall be harmed, for I will wade to my knees in blood in your behalf." The man, a stranger to Mary at the time, was Heber C. Kimball, Apostle, counselor to Brigham Young in the First Presidency of the Church, and grandfather of President Spencer W. Kimball. Elder Kimball's vow to protect Mary was immediately seconded by another bystander, Hyrum Smith, brother of the Prophet Joseph.

Mary courageously stood by her promise to remain with the Saints. In future years she would need this same kind of courage many times in confrontations with unfriendly settlers and mobs.

The Lightners moved numerous times during their marriage, each time seeking better employment and more favorable living conditions. But in spite of their seeking, they experienced many frustrations and hardships. They moved to Lexington, Kentucky, to live with a relative, only to find he had moved north. That left them with no place to live and no work. Mary made men's shirts for fifteen cents apiece, gave painting lessons, and sold some of her own artwork to support the family. While they were living in Farmington, Iowa, Mary's husband's lime kiln burned to the ground, and after painstakingly saving $100 they lost it in a bank failure. Soon after that, they rejoined the Saints in Nauvoo, Illinois, but still had difficulty finding work. When the Prophet Joseph Smith heard they were planning to move again, he told them that the decision to leave would be disastrous:

> Joseph felt very sad when he knew we were going to leave, and with tears running down his cheeks he prophesied that if we left and got away from the Church we would have plenty of sorrow; that we would make property on the right and lose it on the left; that we would have sickness and lose our children; that I would have to work harder than I ever dreamed of and then added, "And at last when you are worn out and old you will get back to the Church."

Joseph's words proved prophetic. While they were in Pontusuc, north of Nauvoo, an infant son, George, was taken sick and died; Mary became very ill and twice nearly died before recovering slowly; their log home was struck by lightning, destroying the structure and severely injuring several members of the family. They agreed to accept a barrel of pork in return for a man's five-hundred-dollar debt to them, only to open the barrel and find the meat spoiled and full of weevils.

Shortly after they moved to St. Croix Falls, Wisconsin, to manage a hotel, Mary's husband and one of their children were critically ill for two weeks. During this time Mary worked day and night caring for sick ones until her feet were so swollen and infected that they almost had to be amputated.

One of Mary's greatest trials came when an elderly gentleman, claiming to be a doctor, gave the family a root that supposedly had healing powers. After five members of the family tasted the root, Mary's two young sons, ages ten and three, died within an hour. Her aunt had convulsions for a period of two weeks, and Mary and her husband, Adam, barely recovered.

The false doctor was captured, nearly hanged by a posse, and finally jailed. He escaped with the help of a friend but was caught in a snowstorm and nearly froze to death before being discovered by Indians. His feet were so severely frostbitten that they were amputated. The capture of the doctor and his suffering, however, provided little comfort for the Lightner family. Their destitution became worse with the death of newly purchased livestock, the theft of many of their possessions, more sickness, and poor diet. Shortly thereafter they paid thousands of dollars to purchase a hotel in Minnesota, but soon lost both hotel and money due to the onset of the American Civil War between the North and the South.

Finally, in 1863 they decided to join Mary's brother, James Henry, who had gone to Utah with the Saints. They traveled by steamboat to Florence, Nebraska, and there joined a large body of Latter-day Saint converts from Europe on their way to Utah. Using a team sent to them by relatives in Utah, the Lightners arrived in the Salt Lake Valley in September 1863.

Mary had a joyful reunion with her brother and mother, whom she had not seen in twenty years, and then traveled south with her husband and ten children to settle in Minersville, Beaver County, Utah, two hundred miles south of Salt Lake City. Adam found plenty of work as a carpenter, and Mary sewed (she was in great demand as a buttonhole maker) and taught school, for which she was paid in vegetables.

Mary was largely responsible for the organization of the Relief Society in Minersville and served as its first president.

Mary testified many times in her later life of how literally Joseph Smith's prophecy of the Lightner family's troubles and eventual prosperity had been fulfilled. In spite of the hardships she had suffered, it was further evidence to her that he was indeed a prophet of God, a testimony she first received as a twelve-year-old girl in Kirtland, Ohio.

Mary Elizabeth Rollins Lightner died December 17, 1913, in Minersville, Utah, at the age of ninety-five.

2

Elizabeth Haven Barlow

From Massachusetts to Mormondom

Two young missionaries, Brigham Young and Willard Richards, were preaching the news of a "restored gospel" through several New England states in 1837 when they stopped in Massachusetts to see their uncle, John Haven, a preacher in the Congregational church in Holliston. With his wife Betsey, John had raised their seven children to observe strict Puritan standards.

John was skeptical of the message Young and Richards brought —a new religion based on heavenly messengers, revelations, and a new "Book of Mormon," said to have been translated from gold plates by a man they called a "prophet," Joseph Smith.

But John's twenty-six-year-old daughter Elizabeth listened attentively to her cousins. She anxiously secluded herself in her bedroom for the next several days, reading the strange new book of scripture the missionaries had left. Within a week she emerged, announcing to her astonished father that she had received a true "religious experience." After much prayer and study, she knew for herself that the Book of Mormon was divine.

Although her father and stepmother were opposed to her desire to join the fledgling church, Elizabeth had been raised to think for herself and search the scriptures for truth.

Elizabeth's interest in religion was certainly not new. As a young teenager, she often hurried to finish her after-school chores and would then steal upstairs and delve into a large chest filled with her ancestors' relics. Among the treasures were unusual old stamps, books, and century-old papers and letters. Because her forebears on both sides were Puritans in the strictest sense, most of the letters and books were very religious in tone. But Elizabeth didn't mind, since she admitted to being "of a religious nature." Her favorite was an old English Bible which her Haven ancestors had brought from England in 1645. Her father had always encouraged Bible reading in his home, and Elizabeth had developed a love for Bible stories and an excellent knowledge of the Savior's life. Because of this, she had been called to teach Sunday School at an early age.

Within a few weeks of Elizabeth's personal conversion to Mormonism, Elder Parley P. Pratt, an Apostle, visited the Haven home and baptized her. Her older sister Nancy and her brother Jesse also joined, and the trio spent hour after hour discussing the Book of Mormon and Joseph Smith.

Early in her teenage years, Elizabeth became skilled in various types of handiwork. She spent many hours around the fire at home weaving straw hats for both men and women, and she became a clever seamstress. Such artistic abilities provided income and would benefit her and her fellow Saints the rest of her life. Elizabeth also made beautiful pin laces and other delicate trimmings. A particular fad of the time was braiding. Elizabeth astonished many friends with her ability to braid fifteen strands at a time and then handle forty-five strands while designing beautiful diamonds and other figures for decorations. With the income brought in by her various talents and by strict economizing, Elizabeth was able to fulfill one of her heart's grandest desires: she sent herself to the Amherst and Bradford colleges near Boston and received a teacher's diploma.

Despite the many opportunities to teach and sell her handiwork in her native Massachusetts, Elizabeth's dream was to meet the Prophet Joseph Smith and live among the Saints who were gathering in Missouri. So in the spring of 1838, Elizabeth, along with her brother Jesse and their nine-year-old niece, Ellen Rockwood, said good-bye to loved ones and the old family home and struck out fifteen hundred miles for Far West, Caldwell County, Missouri. The thirty-day journey was long and hard, but young Elizabeth, Jesse, and Ellen buoyed themselves with dreams of their participation (with the Saints) in building a "New Jerusalem" and a holy temple in Missouri.

During the previous two years, more than 4,900 Saints had poured into the county, seeking refuge from the vicious mobs and persecutions that had driven them from Jackson and Clay counties. In Far West, the Saints had soon built more than 150 homes, four dry-goods stores, three family grocery stores, several blacksmith shops, two hotels, a printing shop, and a large schoolhouse that doubled as a church and courthouse. It was here that Elizabeth had a chance to contribute to her newfound "family" of Saints. Her missionary-cousin Brigham Young, an Apostle in the Church, knew of her college training and soon had arranged for her and Jesse to teach school. The journal of another Far West resident records that Elizabeth "was a very sweet woman beloved by all her scholars and all who became acquainted with her."

Elizabeth, her brother, and her niece were delighted to find the Saints to be exactly as anticipated—hopeful, buoyant, optimistic, and full of a desire to live lives of wholesome righteousness. There were music, drama, debating, hiking, boating, athletics, parties, dancing, and picnics—numerous opportunities for expanding their lives and potentials. The Prophet Joseph Smith, Elizabeth was glad to discover, was not a sanctimonious person who went around with a grave demeanor, as many so-called religious persons in New England did, but one who enjoyed the mental, cultural, and physical aspects of life and encouraged his followers to do the same. He was a warm, affectionate, and engaging personality—a leader who could be both serious and playful. He was someone people enjoyed being around.

This spirit of religious enjoyment, however, was not destined to last long in Missouri. There was inevitable conflict between the Saints and the "old settlers." In October of 1838, less than six months after Elizabeth and her brother arrived in Far West, Governor Lilburn Boggs issued his infamous "Order of Extermination." Within three days, the most brutal massacre of Saints in the history of the Church took place just a few miles from where Elizabeth was living. Two hundred men of the state militia attacked a tiny settlement of thirty families at Haun's Mill. Although the defenseless Saints cried out for peace, the mob fired mercilessly as men and women fled into a blacksmith shop or into the woods. In all, seventeen Mormons were killed, including one elderly man who was hacked to death. Ten-year-old Sardius Smith was found trembling with fear in the blacksmith shop and was cruelly shot to death.

By the end of October, Far West was surrounded by almost three thousand soldiers; for the next several months the Saints and their leaders lived in constant fear for their lives. The Prophet Joseph and many of the brethren had been jailed in Liberty and Richmond. Elizabeth later described the strife and turmoil they suffered as "better to be imagined than described." Even the Church leaders themselves were not immune from disagreement and misunderstandings; there were many dissenters and excommunications during this time among the most prominent Church members. Elizabeth remembered: "We felt more sorrowful at seeing Apostles leave the Church than we did over our trials and persecutions."

The Saints were forced to leave their homes, stores, school, and shops; fifteen thousand homeless Saints crossed the frozen Mississippi River to Quincy, Illinois. "Many births and deaths took place," wrote Elizabeth, "but had it not been for the relief work of the people of Illinois, hundreds of Saints would have died. Potatoes, cornmeal, flour, bedding, and even clothing were supplied in great quantities, these things having been raised throughout the state by public subscription."

But Quincy was to be only a temporary refuge for Elizabeth and the Saints, for the Church soon obtained a large parcel of land in Commerce, Illinois. It was soon renamed "Nauvoo" by Joseph Smith and promoted as the new central gathering place for the harried Saints.

For Elizabeth, the short stay in Quincy was an important one, signaling a new beginning in her life. It was here that she met Israel Barlow, a stalwart man of thirty-three who had joined the Church in 1832 and "had proved himself true during the trying days of Zion's Camp." Israel was immediately attracted to Elizabeth, who had dark eyes and hair and was said to be "a model of form and beauty." They were married on February 23, 1840, and soon moved to Nauvoo, continuing together a life of work and joyful service. Her father, stepmother, and two other children in the family eventually joined the Church, and they enjoyed a happy reunion in Nauvoo.

An important organizational facility for religious, cultural, and social enjoyment in Nauvoo was the "Female Relief Society," organized on March 17, 1842. Elizabeth, one of the early members of this society, attended regularly after her induction on April 28. The purpose of this society, as explained by the Prophet in Elizabeth's hearing, was to look after the wants of the poor and to correct the morals and strengthen the virtues of the community. Members of the society collected donations for the poor, arranged for the helpless to have their gardens plowed and wood chopped, agreed to boycott persons who did not pay poor widows what they owed them, and donated their own handiwork to those in need. They listened to sermons by Church leaders and their own members, administered to the sick, and sought to cultivate all worthy virtues. Elizabeth and her fellow Relief Society sisters were encouraged to be charitable, to cultivate forgiveness, to conduct their lives so as to enjoy gifts of the Spirit, and to spread happiness and goodwill among the Saints. Elizabeth remained active in the Relief Society throughout her life and took pride in being one of those who received instruction directly from the Prophet and from his gracious wife, Emma.

Along with others in Illinois, Elizabeth and her husband Israel migrated to the Salt Lake Valley in 1848 and settled in Bountiful the next year. Elizabeth and her husband found the going "hard." When Israel was called on a mission to England, Elizabeth found herself digging sego roots and thistles and going to the canyon for wood. But they survived the period of hardship.

Elizabeth eventually bore eight children and lived a life of rich satisfaction and accomplishment. She served as president of the East Bountiful Ward Relief Society for thirty-one years, being released at the age of seventy-seven. She enjoyed close association with many of the most prominent women in the Latter-day Saint community, including Eliza R. Snow, Zina D. H. Young, and Mary Fielding Smith.

At her funeral in 1892, speakers quoted one of her favorite scriptures, a passage from Revelation, chapter 7:

> What are these which are arrayed in white robes? . . . And I said unto him, Sir, thou knowest. And he said to me, These are they which came out of great tribulation, and have washed their robes, and made them white in the blood of the Lamb. . . . They shall hunger no more, neither [shall they] thirst . . . and God shall wipe away all tears from their eyes.

3

Drusilla Dorris Hendricks

"Mother's Little Christian"

Drusilla Dorris grew up in Sumner County, Tennessee, not far from the southern border of Kentucky. Born in 1810, the tenth child of William Dorris and Catherine Frost, she was on "the cutting edge" of the frontier. When she was very small, an earthquake shook the region, creating the Reelfoot Lake in northwestern Tennessee. In her seventh year her father sent her to school for six months, where she learned to read and write a little. Because of the lack of books, her reading was confined to the Bible and her church's hymnbook.

When Drusilla was ten she went on an errand for her father and waded a stream of water which caused her to take cold. She came down with a pain in her side and almost died. Although she eventually recovered, the pain settled in her right shoulder, and the doctor took out her collarbone and many other pieces of bone. She was an invalid for two years. During this time she continued to read the Bible and hymnbook. She had a good mind and asked her father and mother many questions about religion and life.

Religion was a preoccupation, but not the only one. The Tennessee woods were filled with squirrels, chinquapins (little chestnuts), honey trees, and sour-tasting persimmons. Her early life consisted not only of work in the house—spinning, weaving, helping her mother cook, and scrubbing the floor—but also picking wild berries, watching the many birds, gathering nuts, and learning the ways of bears, deer, and woodchucks. She helped her father plant and hoe corn and potatoes, plant and pick cotton, pull flax and prepare it to be worked into cloth, and assist with the bellows when he worked in the blacksmith shop.

One time one of Drusilla's friends, Sarah Pea, was traveling with her father from Illinois to Tennessee near Drusilla's home. When they began a long uphill climb, Sarah was let out of the buckboard wagon and told to run on ahead. Every so often Sarah would look back to see how the horses were coming with the wagon. Then she saw what she supposed was a big black dog some distance behind her. Although she thought nothing of it, her father recognized it to be a large black wolf, potentially dangerous. Mr. Pea stopped the wagons, took out one of the horses, and galloped toward Sarah, hoping to scare away the wolf. The wolf was only a few rods behind her when it was frightened by the father's "hallow" and turned into the creek. "When father came up and told me the danger I was in," wrote Sarah, "it was hard to tell which was scared the worst of us three—father, the wolf, or myself."

Perhaps because she had been confined by her illness for important years of her life, Drusilla was a dreamer. She believed that dreams could become reality and that they frequently held messages for her. "I had dreams mostly from my childhood up and had seen many of my dreams literally fulfilled. My mother would call me 'Joseph the Dreamer.' "

Having been born just five years after the Prophet Joseph Smith, Drusilla grew up in the same general religious atmosphere as young Joseph did. The Second Great Awakening, a period of religious excitement and intensity, was sweeping the nation, and one of Drusilla's earliest dreams symbolized one of her concerns:

"I saw Jacob's ladder reaching into heaven, I saw men ascending and descending on it. There were seven steps, it had the appearance of a rainbow, both the steps and uprights. I concluded that there should be more communication between the heavens and earth." Belief in this concept would prepare her to accept readily one of the most important doctrines of Mormonism, that of modern-day revelation.

Drusilla and her family were witnesses to the fiery-tongued preachers, the extreme emotions, and certain physical excesses which characterized many religious meetings. The Puritans, Quakers, Church of England, Presbyterians, Baptists, and Lutherans all gained sizable followings as revivals were held throughout the land. The movement peaked around 1824, when Drusilla was a fourteen-year-old girl and a serious Bible student.

Drusilla's parents were Southerners and members of the Baptist church, but her father soon became disturbed with the rollicking and jerking that came with revival meetings. Their neighbors in Tennessee were Methodists and Presbyterians and Drusilla claims, "I heard much contention among everyone concerning religion."

Drusilla learned to read at the age of seven, the Bible being her only text, and was soon able to quote full pages of scripture. She used scripture so frequently in her day-to-day activities that she soon became the brunt of playful teasing from her brothers and sisters, who called her "Mother's little Christian."

Although she officially joined the Baptist church as a young woman, Drusilla remained frustrated with the way the scriptures were being interpreted by various preachers. "I found that none of the Churches had the gospel as taught in the New Testament. It seemed so strange to me that no one was doing as the Bible told them."

This concern was common among many during the Second Great Awakening. They believed that the primitive New Testament Church had been destroyed in apostasy and that the authority to perform certain ordinances, such as baptism and marriage, had been lost. To many, restoration of the ancient gospel was necessary before the second coming of Christ, which they believed was imminent.

Drusilla was among those who shared such beliefs and therefore was extremely interested when invited by a brother-in-law to go hear two Mormon elders who were in their area preaching a "restored gospel." Her skeptical relative assured her, "You have read so much that you can catch their errors in the scriptures."

But Drusilla came away impressed and "rejoicing, for I believed." After thorough study and spiritual confirmation of her desire to become a Latter-day Saint, she was baptized in 1835. She wrote:

> I shall never forget how I felt. The elder asked if I was willing to serve the Lord to the best of my ability. I answered yes. He then baptized me according to the pattern laid down by our Lord and Savior, Jesus Christ, for the baptism of all those who wished to serve Him. I arose to walk in newness of life. That fear of death and hell was all gone from me and I was a new creature. A feeling of calmness pervaded me for months.

Such peace and tranquility was only to exist within her heart, however, for Drusilla's life would be full of trials and persecutions, which began immediately after her baptism. "We are happy, though high and low scoff at us."

Drusilla's husband, James Hendricks, whom she had married in 1827, was baptized at the same time and they were immediately rejected by members of their families. James's relatives forbade any family members to enter James and Drusilla's home and relatives on both sides scorned them openly in their church meetings, praying for their souls which had surely "gone to the devil." Rocks were hurled at them and their home, and their property was frequently vandalized.

As soon as they were financially able, Drusilla and James began their journey to Clay County, Missouri, where the Saints were gathering. Drusilla recalled that as they left their home in Tennessee, "I had four sisters to leave but only one to regret our leaving. She was a Latter-day Saint." Drusilla had been very close to her sisters while growing up and until her baptism "we never met or parted without crying."

The move to Missouri, however, was to be only the first in a long series of moves they would be forced to make because of their religious beliefs. Within a short time, anti-Mormon mobs forced them to move from Clay to Caldwell County. It was during their stay there in 1838 that James suffered an injury that would cripple him for the rest of his life. Charles C. Rich called at the Hendricks's home late one night to summon James to assist the Mormons against a mob assembled on Crooked River, just a few miles south of where they were living. "Don't get shot in the back," Drusilla said to James as she handed him the gun. The next time she saw him, James was on a bed, a shot in the neck having paralyzed him from the neck down.

Through the moves from Missouri to Quincy, Illinois, to Nauvoo and on towards Winter Quarters, Nebraska, James improved, but nearly all of the responsibility for caring for the family and transporting them from place to place fell upon Drusilla. "I had to lift my husband at least fifty times a day and in doing so I had to strain every nerve," she records. One can imagine this young mother, with five children under the age of ten and a husband in very poor health, caring for her family's daily needs of food and clothing, as well as milking cows, feeding livestock, trying to grow a garden, maintaining their living quarters, and trying to bring in money for supplies by taking in boarders, washing, and sewing. In addition, she strained under the emotional pressure of being surrounded by anti-Mormon sentiment and persecution.

One excerpt from her journal describes her managerial skills:

> I paid $56, for house rent and got me two bedsteads, four chairs, five falling leaf tables. Kept one of the tables myself and let Bro. Lewis have one for moving us to Nauvoo, sold two to Sister Emma Smith for provisions. The brethren gave us a lot and put together a log house and I hired a man to cover it and build a chimney. I and sister Melinda Lewis chinked and plastered it. We raised a good garden. I began to make beer and gingerbread and go out on public days, this showing that necessity is the mother of invention. I paid a good deal of tithing by making gloves and mittens. I had about thirty pair on hand. I still went washing for bread or molasses for my children.

Only Drusilla's oldest son, William, was of much help to his mother. One of her greatest trials was the call he received to join the ranks of the Mormon Battalion. Drusilla wrote how "one would say to me, Is William going? I answered, No he is not. Then another would ask, Is William going? No. Why, they said, they would not have their son or husband stay for anything. Then I would say, a burned child dreads the fire."

Then Drusilla recounts how when she was alone she had second thoughts: "The whispering of the Spirit would say to me: 'Are you afraid to trust the God of Israel? Has He not been with you in all your trials? Has He not provided for your wants?' Then I would have to acknowledge the hand of God in all His goodness to me."

The day of mustering-in dawned, finding Drusilla still adamant. She recorded how William set off for the morning chores:

> My eyes followed him as he started through the tall heavy grass wet with dew. I thought how easy something might happen, for that was a sickly climate. I got ready to get breakfast and when I stepped up on the wagon tongue to get my flour I was asked by the same spirit that had spoken to me before, if I did not want the greatest glory and I answered with my natural voice, Yes, I did. Then how can you get it without making the greatest sacrifices, said the voice. I answered Lord, what lack I yet? Let your son go in the Battalion, said the voice.
>
> I said, It is too late. They are to be marched off this morning. That spirit then left me with the heartache. I got breakfast and called the girls and their Father to come to the tent for prayers. William came— wet with dew from the grass and we sat down around the board and my husband commenced asking the blessing on the food. Then Thomas Williams came shouting at the top of his voice, saying "Turn out men, turn out, for we do not wish to press you but we lack some men yet in the Battalion. William raised his eyes and looked me in the face. I knew then that he would go as well as I know now that he has been. . . . I went to milk the cows. . . . I thought the cows would be shelter for me and I knelt down and told the Lord if He wanted my child to take him, only spare his life. . . . I felt it was all I could do. Then a voice . . . answered me saying, It shall be done unto you as it was unto Abraham when he offered Isaac on the altar. I don't know whether I milked or not for I felt the Lord had spoken to me.

Drusilla's earnest prayer was answered, for William survived the Battalion march and joined his family after they had arrived in the Salt Lake Valley. Together they went on to help settle Cache Valley. William later pioneered in southern Idaho and in Latter-day Saint colonies in northern Mexico.

Drusilla's husband, James, survived the crossing of the Great Plains and became the first bishop of the Salt Lake City Nineteenth Ward, while Drusilla served as Relief Society president. She continued to support her family as well as several grandchildren by taking in boarders and managing the old Warm Springs Bathhouse in northwest Salt Lake City. She wrote during her final years, "The gospel is true. I have rejoiced in it through all my trials for the Spirit of the Lord has buoyed me up or I should have failed."

Here are revealed the inner thoughts and life of one woman and the effect of her strength on one family and on the Church. Brigham

Young was extremely complimentary of the role of such women in pioneering the west and establishing Zion. "If the women did not accomplish as much as the men did," he said, it was because the women "had no wives to help them."

Drusilla Dorris Hendricks died in Richmond, Cache County, Utah at the age of seventy-one. She is buried there along with her husband, who had died eleven years earlier.

4

Jane Snyder Richards
Strong of Will and Spirit

Nearly three hundred people gathered on the shore of Lake La Porte, Indiana, on a cold day in January of 1840. Word had spread quickly through the nearby communities that Robert Snyder, a young "Mormonite" missionary, intended to baptize his sixteen-year-old sister that day in the icy waters. Jane Snyder had been seriously ill for several weeks and the townspeople were appalled that her older brother would risk her life to baptize her under such circumstances.

Just the day before, Jane had awakened unable to speak, paralyzed and apparently close to death. But through the prayers and sacred anointings of her older brother, she regained her speech and was freed of the severe pain she had been suffering. Then, for the first time, she expressed a desire to be baptized a member of The Church of Jesus Christ of Latter-day Saints. Jane described the effects of her brother's prayer:

> While he was praying, a light came into my mind, and I saw as plainly as if a book were opened before me with it written in it, my need of baptism—if Christ who was sinless needed to be baptized, should I hold myself as better than He? As my brother arose from his knees, I showed him my restored arm and hand, and begged for baptism. He remonstrated, for it was now midwinter and ice would have to be

broken and the exposure might be fatal. But death I was not afraid of, only I must be baptized.

Wrapped in a woolen blanket and armed with complete faith in God, Jane was carried to the lake the next day. The crowd, mostly hostile, shouted abuses at Robert as he broke through nearly a foot of ice to prepare for the ordinance. Some threatened to arrest the missionary-brother if he immersed his weak and sickly sister in the freezing water.

Robert let himself down into the opening in the ice and his brother George assisted Jane into the water. "Without a tremor" she went in and was "buried with Christ by baptism." Immediately upon coming out of the water Jane declared in a loud and confident voice:

> I want to say to all you people who have come out to see me baptized, that I do it of my own free will and choice, and if you interfere with the man who has baptized me, God will interfere with you.

She later wrote of the incident:

> I was a diffident girl and all my family was astonished to hear me speak in this manner. I did not know what I was saying, but they told me afterwards.

The crowd quietly dispersed without harming Elder Snyder, and Jane emerged from the baptismal service healed of her illness rather than suffering any harm.

Such was the strong-willed determination and spiritual strength of Jane Snyder. Although some considered her stubborn independence somewhat unladylike, her inner strength proved able to carry her through the many hardships and trials she would experience during her lifetime.

Jane was born January 31, 1823, the tenth of eleven children of Isaac and Lovisa Comstock Snyder. Jane's father, a native of Vermont, was a prosperous farmer and stockraiser. He led an exemplary life but was affiliated with no particular religion. Her mother, originally from Massachusetts, was a devout Methodist.

Jane was born in the little town of Pamelia, Jefferson County, New York. However, the family was living in East Camden in the province of Ontario, Canada, when they first became acquainted with Mormonism. Jane's older brother, Robert, had been seriously ill with consumption (tuberculosis) for nearly three years, spending two of those years secluded in his bedroom meditating and studying the scriptures.

One night while in prayer for guidance to the truth, Robert heard a still, small voice distinctly whisper a name to him—John E. Page. Two weeks later, two Mormon missionaries held a preaching service within two miles of the Snyder home. Among the many people the elders converted and baptized was a married sister of Robert and Jane Snyder. When the Snyder family received word of her baptism, Robert immediately inquired as to the names of the two missionaries. One of the elders was indeed John E. Page, a future Apostle in the newly organized church. As soon as Robert was baptized and administered to by Elder Page, the illness he had suffered for three years, up to that point considered incurable, left him. Robert, twenty-three, became a missionary himself for five years, baptizing hundreds in the United States and Canada, including all the Snyder family except Jane and her younger brother, Jesse.

Although Jane was impressed with her brother's improved health, she stubbornly resisted baptism. "What sins have I committed?" she asked her pleading brother. "Have I not always obeyed my parents?" But her attitude was clearly changed by the illness she suffered during the winter of 1839-1840. It nearly took her life and was cured only upon her baptism. Her brother died two years later, in 1842, "in full faith of the gospel, feeling that his work was done."

Jane was fourteen and not yet a member of the Church when her family followed the counsel of Church leaders and sold their property in Canada and began the trek west to join other Saints gathering in Missouri. The trip was interrupted in La Porte, Indiana, on account of the illness of Jane's little niece, Sara Jane. Upon her recovery, they again made plans to move on when they received word from the Prophet Joseph Smith himself that he wished them to remain in Indiana another two years to provide a home for Mormon missionaries as they traveled through the state.

Finally, in the fall of 1841, the family was at liberty to migrate. By this time, angry mobs had driven the Saints out of Missouri and the new gathering place was Nauvoo, Illinois, a Mormon settlement of a few thousand Saints on the east bank of the Mississippi River.

In Nauvoo, Jane first saw Joseph Smith, the Prophet. She described her feelings:

I recognized him from a dream I had had. He had such an angelic countenance as I never saw before. Then he was 37 years of age. His hair was of a light-brown, blue eyes, and light-complexioned. His natural demeanor was quiet; his character and disposition was formed by his life work; he was kind and considerate, taking a personal interest in all his people, considering everyone his equal. We were regular in our attendance at the meetings, and were always anxious to hear Brother Joseph.

Jane also became acquainted with several other men who were to be prominent in the history of the Church: Brigham Young, Heber C. Kimball, Willard Richards, John Taylor, Wilford Woodruff, George A. Smith, and many others.

Jane was nineteen when she married Franklin D. Richards, a missionary whom she had met when he and his companion, Elder Jehiel Savage, stopped with her family in La Porte, Indiana, on their way to Canada. Elder Richards was unable to complete the mission due to poor health, and he and Jane were married December 18, 1842 at Job Creek, near La Porte, Hancock County, Illinois. Jane's brother Samuel performed the wedding ceremony and the couple soon made their home on Young Street in Nauvoo.

Although Jane had already experienced much sickness and many hardships, none would compare with the trials that still lay before her. Anti-Mormon persecutions soon made it necessary for the Saints to leave Nauvoo and seek refuge in the Rocky Mountains. Jane, her husband Franklin, and their daughter Wealthy, born in 1843, started west in 1846. They sold their nearly completed two-story brick home in order to buy supplies for the journey. Within three weeks, however, Franklin was called on a proselyting mission to England. Jane, pregnant with their second child, was so feeble and ill that she felt she might not live to see her husband's return. It was a sad parting for the little family.

On July 23, 1846, twenty days after Franklin left for England, Jane gave birth to a son, Isaac Phineas, who died within an hour. She was assisted in the delivery by a midwife who had been summoned from five miles away. Upon completion of her duties, the midwife inquired, "Are you prepared to pay me?"

"If it were to save my life," answered Jane, near death, "I could not give you any money, for I have none; but if you see anything you want, take it."

With that, the woman picked up a beautiful woolen bedspread worth fifteen dollars. "I may as well take it, for you'll never live to see it," was her cold remark, and she left Jane desperately ill with her dead baby at her side. Jane could not bear the thought of burying the child on the prairie where the grave might be molested, so she and Grandmother Snyder carried the child with them until they reached Mt. Pisgah, Iowa, where he could be buried more decently.

Jane's only other child, two-year-old Wealthy, had become ill about the time her father left and was becoming weaker as the journey progressed. En route to the Missouri River, they passed a large potato field and little Wealthy asked for a potato. Her grandmother Snyder went to the nearby farmhouse to ask if they could buy some potatoes. The owner bitterly replied, "I wouldn't sell or give one of you damned Mormons a potato to save your lives." She then sent the dog after Mrs. Snyder. When Wealthy was tearfully told of the incident she replied, "Never mind, mama, she's a wicked woman, isn't she? We wouldn't do that by her, would we?"

As Jane and Wealthy's conditions worsened, Brigham Young received word of their situation and rode back some fifty miles to counsel with them. Upon visiting with the family, he said that had he been aware of their difficulties sooner, he would not have asked Franklin to go on his mission.

Two months after she buried her infant son, Jane's little girl, not yet three years old, died and was buried at Cutler's Park, near the bank of the Missouri River.

At twenty-three, Jane was now childless and without the aid and comfort of her husband. She spent a harsh winter at Winter Quarters, Nebraska, where she gained back some of her strength in spite of scanty provisions.

Jane's husband returned from his mission in the spring of 1848 and that summer they crossed the Great Plains to the Salt Lake Valley, arriving the nineteenth of October. The journey took three and a half months, during two of which Jane was confined to her bed because of illness.

Franklin Richards was soon called to become a member of the Council of the Twelve Apostles; this increased his responsibilities and took him away from home frequently to supervise foreign missions and to preside over Church meetings in other areas. In fact,

Elder Richards was away from home ten of the first fifteen years he and Jane were married. Jane later remarked that she became so accustomed to his being away that when he was home she occasionally forgot to call him to the table at mealtime.

Jane eventually had four more children—Franklin S., Josephine, Lorenzo Maeser, and Charles Comstock, all of whom grew to adulthood and became faithful members of the Church and contributing members of their communities.

In 1868, Franklin and Jane moved to Ogden, where Jane played a prominent role in the Relief Society. In 1872 she became president of a ward Relief Society in Ogden, and in 1877 President Brigham Young called her to preside over the Weber Stake Relief Societies. It marked the first time a stake Relief Society organization had been created in the Church.

Eleven years later Jane was called to become first counselor to Zina D. H. Young, general president of the Relief Society organization of the Church. At the age of sixty-eight, Jane accompanied Sarah M. Kimball and Emmeline B. Wells to attend the National Council of Women, meeting in Washington, D.C.

Jane had several opportunities to travel throughout the country with her husband and children. In 1880, she and Franklin journeyed to the eastern and midwestern United States and visited places important in early Church history. During this trip they took time to identify the spot on the banks of the Missouri River where their little daughter Wealthy had been buried thirty-four years earlier.

Jane, who enjoyed doing temple work, was proud of having performed ordinances for the dead in nearly all the temples built by the Saints during her lifetime. She attended the dedication of each temple except the Logan Temple.

In her later life Jane continued to combine her activities as an independent and outspoken woman with respect for Church authorities. She also had a reputation for being a peacemaker and was a natural and skillful nurse. Benevolent and charitable by nature, Jane was unexcelled as a comforter of the sick and the sorrowful. Speaking at a Relief Society general conference in 1904, Jane encouraged the sisters to visit the sick and those in need "rather than idly taking tea with the neighbors." She said that one should even miss her meetings, if necessary, to take the sick or elderly out for a ride.

Jane Snyder Richards passed away at the home of her daughter, November 17, 1913, at the age of ninety. Her funeral was one of the largest ever held in the Ogden Tabernacle; speakers included some of the most prominent men and women in the Church, including President Joseph F. Smith, David O. McKay, and Relief Society general president Emmeline B. Wells.

Charles Comstock Richards, her youngest son, later spoke to a group of Relief Society sisters, summing up the positive effects Jane's suffering had on her personality and character:

> Mother's trials and hardships increased her capacity for human sympathy and prepared her for the labor of love awaiting her, and which she cheerfully performed, in the Relief Society organizations and in other capacities. Patient in misfortune, sympathetic, generous and helpful to others in sorrow and distress, she bestowed blessings upon thousands less fortunate than herself, in whose hearts her memory is lovingly enshrined.

5

Rachel Emma Woolley Simmons
Twelve-year-old Teamster Who Crossed the Plains

Rachel Emma Woolley was only twelve years old when she climbed onto the driver's seat of one of her family's covered wagons just a few miles from Winter Quarters, Nebraska. She took a deep breath, snapped the reins, and drove the first of the more than one thousand miles she would drive to the Salt Lake Valley. Hers was one of nearly four hundred wagons crossing the Great Plains in 1848 under the direction of Brigham Young.

Born in 1836 in Columbia County, Ohio, the daughter of Edwin D. Woolley and Mary Wickersham, Rachel was three years old when her Quaker parents joined the Church in East Rochester, Ohio.

Rachel found the trek across the plains to be a great adventure, full of fun times with her young companions, but she was not very pleased when the young man her father had hired to drive one of the wagons deserted just a few days after their exodus from Winter Quarters. That left Rachel to contend with the frisky team. "I did so with fear and trembling, as one of the horses was very vicious. She used to kick up dreadful until she would kick the board of the wagon all to pieces, but it made no difference, I had to go at it the next day just the same."

Rachel had spent much of that spring helping the family prepare for the "Great Migration to the Valley." Farms plowed the previous year had produced abundantly, and branches of the Church in the East and in England had sent generous donations of clothing and money with returning missionaries. Such assistance helped the Woolleys and other families fill their wagons with supplies for the four-month journey.

Rachel's father had two wagons, one buggy, and a "light spring wagon" made into a comfortable bed for her mother, who was seven months pregnant. Supplies to sustain their family of ten included 2,000 pounds of flour, 40 pounds of sugar, several hundred pounds of other foods, a rifle and ammunition, and a thousand pounds of bedding, cooking gear, and clothing and personal belongings. They also took along nine yoke of oxen, two horses, beef cattle, several milk cows, sheep, and a pregnant sow.

For Rachel and most of the others, the first two or three weeks were the most difficult, although the roads would become rougher further west. "For miles and miles one could see nothing but the unbroken plains. Not a tree or a shrub in sight, nothing but the white dusty road as far as the eye could see." In addition, it took time for the travelers' minds and bodies to adjust to endless walking, little sleep, the petty irritations of travel, and the need for constant alertness to physical dangers.

Even as evening fell there was little rest to be had by some. Wolves "kicked up a regular rumpus" during the night, dogs barked, cattle lowed, and men had to dress and go out to comfort them by speaking softly.

Rachel was greatly relieved each afternoon as the camp was reached. Then she and her companions "always made a rush for the river (Platte) to bathe. It was great enjoyment after the warm dusty day."

Rachel's bathing parties did not always have a pleasant ending, however:

> I had one of the most indulgent of mothers, but she had told me many times not to go in bathing so often, but I was disobedient and went with the girls as usual after the many warnings I had received. We staid longer than usual and the night being very dark I lost my way. I suppose I must have passed the wagons and not recognized them. The grass was very high and the dew very heavy. I was wet to my knees, but after what seemed to me a very long time, and after I had repented my disobedience, I found our wagons and also found Father with a rope in

his hand waiting to receive me. I received a deserved warm reception. I think it had the desired effect. I don't remember any more escapades of that kind during the rest of the journey. In consequence of getting so wet that night, I had a crick in my neck the next morning. My head was drawn on one side. I tried to make myself believe it was because Father had whipped me and thought he ought to be sorry, but it didn't seem to strike him that way. I had to lie in bed all day. Mother petted me some, I remember. Disagreeable results always follow disobedience whether in young or old.

As the company progressed, they entered the vast buffalo range. Because of the flatness of the country, they could see thousands of buffalo in one glance. Sometimes the animals would string out in a long train a mile or more in length. Running at a sort of coyote lope, they made the ground tremble beneath the tramp of their hoofs, with a noise resembling thunder. As one of Rachel's companions wrote, "Woe be unto the wagon train if our trail of wagons was in the direct line of their march. Stop they would not. These noble animals had been accustomed from time immemorial to the right of way and they would go, helter skelter, pell mell, through and over wagons and outfits, breaking, crashing and scattering wagons, goods, utensils, and leaving destruction in their trail."

But the buffalo were welcomed because they furnished fuel, something that was now in critically short supply due to the lack of timber. The euphemism "buffalo chips" for dried buffalo dung did little, as Hosea Stout said, to lessen "the rather unfavorable impression on our women, relative to being entirely confined to them before we got to our journey's end." In spite of its odor, the stuff burned brightly and intensely, turning to embers much more rapidly than wood did. As her family neared each night's campground, Rachel would jump out of the wagon, "take a sack and fill it as our journey progressed." One evening the chips were "very thick in a certain place close to the road, which was not often the case, as there were so many ahead of us. I thought I was in luck, but I soon found out the cause. I was picking up as fast as I could when all at once I heard the rattle of a snake. I looked to see in what direction it was and there he was in a hole almost at my feet. I did not stop for any more chips at that time."

The Fourth of July arrived, finding the Woolleys with "only corn-dodger and buffalo meat" to celebrate with. Rachel's Aunt Catherine had all of Rachel's family over for a noodle soup dinner, after which they "made a rise" and had a chance to dance.

Rachel's mother, Mary, could tell that her new baby was ready to come; the next day her painless contractions turned to hard labor. Rachel helped in carrying water and coal to the wagon as a midwife helped ease Mary's discomfort by rubbing her back, fetching water for her thirst, brewing herb tea to ease the pain, and talking to her quietly to help her relax. Soon the cry of a newborn baby was heard outside the wagon, and the family rejoiced. Rachel had a new baby sister who weighed in at ten and one-half pounds. The baby received her mother's name, Mary, and would grow up to become the mother of J. Reuben Clark, Jr., a prominent American diplomat and a member of the First Presidency of The Church of Jesus Christ of Latter-day Saints.

Rachel wrote:

> We never laid over a day in consequence of mother's sickness. The Lord blessed her and fitted her to bear the journey as He did many others at that time. I have heard her say she never got along better in her life. Mary grew so fast, she was one of Mother's finest children, even if she was born under difficulties.

Just a few weeks later, another addition was made to the Woolley family—their sow had a litter of three piglets. Rachel remembered the bad day on Rocky Ridge in Wyoming:

> I was driving as usual and to make matters worse we had an old pig that was in trouble that day and she had to ride in the buggy, as Father was very anxious to save the little pigs, but they all died in consequence of the rough road. I remember I was so glad when we camped that night, because I was so completely tired out with the road and the frisky horse.

Not all of the journey was tedium. One day in seven was a rest day, with worship service held on the prairie. After meeting, Rachel helped wash clothes and picked greens and gooseberries. The men made repairs, and from a bridge boys threw lumps of dirt at the garfish. Others hiked over to an abandoned Indian village. In the evening, under a bright moon, parents chatted and swatted mosquitos while the younger ones chased fireflies.

The company in which Rachel traveled did not experience the high number of deaths that companies before them had suffered, or the handcart companies which would come later in 1856, but that did not lessen the heartache felt by all as a loved one succumbed to the rigors of the trip. A young boy drowned and a mother died of measles, but the death that affected the pioneers perhaps most intensely involved a tragedy against which they constantly warned their children. Mary Ann Weston Maughan wrote:

> About noon as we were traveling along on a good plain road, my little Peter, about three years old, was sitting in the front of the wagon between his brother Charles and his sister Mary Ann. They were looking at a cow that had lost one horn. He leaned forward, lost his balance, and fell before the wheels. The first passed over him and he tried to escape the other one. But alas the wagon stopped just as the hind wheel stood on his dear little back. The Brethren from behind ran up and lifted the wheel and took him from under it. He was bruised internally so that it was impossible for him to live long. We done all that was possible, but no earthly power could save him. He did not suffer much pain, really. The people left their wagons and gathered around mine, and all wept for the dear little boy that we knew must soon leave us.
>
> I had talked to him many times to be careful and not fall out of the wagon, or he might be hurt very bad. I did not know that his father had fainted, for the Brethren stood to hide him from my sight. On my asking for him, they said he would come soon. As soon as he was able he came to the wagon, covered with dust. But his little boy could not speak to him. He opened his eyes and looked so lovingly at us, then gently closed them and passed peacefully away, and left us weeping around his dear little bruised body. Then loving hands tenderly dressed him in a suit of his own white clothes. He looked so lovely. I emptied a dry goods box and Brother Wood made him a nice coffin; and it even was a mournful satisfaction, for we had seen our brothers and sisters bury their dear ones without a coffin to lay them in.
>
> We buried him on a little hill on the North side of the road. The grave was consecrated and then they laid him to rest. Some one had made a nice headboard, with his name printed on, also his age and date of death. This was all we could do, and many prayers were offered to our Heavenly Father, that he might rest in peace and not be disturbed. We turned away in sorrow and grief.

The wagon train soon left the prairie and began climbing the pass through the Rocky Mountains. There, during the night of July 26, the company experienced the first sharp frost. The mountain trail was up and down hills, rocky, and very hard on the cattle's feet. Many of the travelers came down with mountain fever, so layovers were longer and more frequent. But the Saints were far from discouraged. They found pine wood, which made a roaring fire; they hunted antelope and buffalo; and the fishing in the clear streams was excellent. Not toothache, or cut finger, or broken axle could break their spirits, for they were in the mountains of the Lord. Rachel wrote, "We were so near our journey's end that we actually rejoiced. . . ."

From the summit of Big Mountain, Rachel caught her first glimpse of the southern part of their promised valley. On September 22, after four months on the trail, many in the company arose at five o'clock to get an early start entering the valley. By noon, Rachel remembers, they camped at the mouth of Emigration Canyon "to wash and fix up a little before meeting friends that had preceded us the year before."

As the wagons limped into the valley, Rachel's Uncle John and his wife, who had arrived the previous year, were there to greet them with a hot vegetable dinner. "I have no doubt," Rachel wrote, "but what we did justice to that supper, being the first in a house for five months." They pitched their tents in a friend's backyard, hugged all their relatives, and went to bed.

At the age of fifteen Rachel married Joseph M. Simmons; they became the parents of ten children, living in Grantsville, in northwestern Utah. Left a widow at thirty-five, she became a practicing midwife to support her large family.

Just as Rachel had kept a good record of her experiences crossing the plains in 1848, she continued her journal until recording her last entry in 1891, unaware that she would live another thirty-five remarkable years. Her journal bears record of a difficult life filled with small triumphs in her service to others, in her success at keeping the Word of Wisdom (she had vowed in 1881 to abstain from tea and coffee), and in her efforts to "live a life of usefulness and do the work the Lord has given me to do in meekness and humility."

Upon Rachel's death in 1926 at age ninety, her daughter wrote of her: "I do not think a better woman ever lived. From my earliest recollection she has been everything that is noble, brave, self-sacrificing, loving, hard working, staunch and true to every principle of the Gospel, teaching her children the same, both by precept and example."

Part Two

Four Who Crossed
the Ocean

6

Patience Loader Rozsa Archer

The Englishwoman Who Walked to Zion

From the deck of the sailing vessel *John J. Boyd,* James and Amy Loader anxiously scanned the dock at Liverpool, England, looking for their twenty-eight-year-old daughter, Patience. The baggage of the Loader family had been carried aboard the day before, and the captain had said they would leave for New York City the next afternoon.

Now, with little warning, he announced that they were to sail earlier than expected, and Patience had not yet returned from visiting her sister who lived nearby. Just as the crew was taking up the last gangplank, Patience's mother spotted her making her way through the crowd. She shouted for her to hurry and pleaded with the sailors to let her daughter aboard. Only one narrow plank remained connecting the dock to the deck of the ship. James and Amy watched anxiously as two sailors helped Patience cross the plank, one walking in front and one behind, the deep water below them lapping against the ship and the dock. After a seemingly endless time, she made it safely aboard and was greeted with cheers and hugs from her family.

This tense moment was the beginning of an incredible year-long journey that would take the Loader family thousands of miles by ship, rail, wagon, handcart, and foot from their English homeland to the Salt Lake Valley.

Patience was born August 23, 1827, in Aston Rouant, Oxford-shire, a small village nestled in the green, rolling hills of southern England. The Loader family lived only fifteen miles from Oxford, home of the famous university, and Patience heard much about that school during her early years.

Patience's father, James Loader, served for twenty-three years as head gardener for Sir Henry Lambert, an English nobleman of high rank. This position afforded the thirteen Loader children the privilege of attending school with the nobleman's family. Their education, therefore, was better than that of many of their playmates, and the family's lifestyle was somewhat more comfortable. Each year at Christmastime, for example, Queen Victoria visited the school and gave each child a small plum pudding.

Patience's childhood home, which she described as "enchanting," had a steep thatched roof, cut-glass windows, and a veranda laced with vines, climbing roses, and honeysuckle blossoms. The red-brick walk leading to the Loader home, kept free of all weeds and stray grass, was framed on each side by a beautiful flower garden. Each child was given her own tiny plot of ground and was furnished seeds and tools with which to grow her own fruit-and-vegetable garden. A gravel walkway wound around the side of the cottage to a miniature playground in back where Patience and the other children played with balls and bats, jumped ropes, and laughed through hundreds of games of tag and "Ring Around the Rosie." James Loader tried to provide amusements for his children at home so they would not need to seek them in the streets or other less desirable places.

In the evenings, James and Amy gathered their family together in front of the coal-burning stove and told tales, both true and home-spun, of English heroes. The deeds of King Henry VIII, Lord Nelson, the Duke of Wellington, King Arthur and the Round Table, and Robin Hood were described to an eager audience. After all, Patience grew up just one hundred miles from Sherwood Forest.

The Loader family belonged to the Church of England, and Patience was brought up in strict accordance with its teachings. She wrote:

> Never can I remember being put to bed without having to kneel at my dear Mother's knee to say my prayers and to ask God to take care of me through the night. We was all taught . . . that we was depending on

God our Heavenly Father for all we was blessed with, and we was taught to thank Him for all blessings in my early life.

As a young woman, Patience grew weary of the endless number of meetings she had to sit through each Sunday. She thought of religion as "long-faced" and wished instead that she could go for "a nice walk with . . . friends or sometimes go visiting." Nevertheless, she deeply appreciated her religious training.

As Patience grew up, she developed a spirit of independence. At the age of seventeen, she expressed a desire to set out on her own, find a job, and earn her own living. Many elderly couples, hotels, and other business establishments hired young girls to do washing, cooking, cleaning, and other housework. Although the pay was minimal, Patience was excited when she found such an arrangement with two women who ran a boarding school several miles from Aston Rouant. She described her feelings as the day approached for her to leave home to work:

> I thought this was verey grand for me to work and earn my own living. I was verey anxious to do this. But when I thought of leaving my home, father and mother, Brs. & sisters and all, in my own mind I came nearly backing out and not go. Then as I had been so anxious to work out, my independent spirit would not let me tell my parents that I did not want to go. If I had said I would not or did not want to as my Father would have been glad for me to stay home . . . [but] I thought he had worked for me long enough.

The day before Patience was to report for work at the boarding school, her older sister Lois talked her into going to a fair being held a few miles away. Fairs were common in England, but Patience's mother and father had never allowed her to go to one. The urge to steal away and have fun was tempting. When Patience's parents left the house for a short time, therefore, she and her sister crept through the backyard, squeezed through the thick shrubs, scaled a high wooden fence, and "escaped." They did not dare go through the village for fear of running into their mother or father, but instead took another road out of town. Patience's loyalty to her parents and her basically obedient spirit are evident in her description of her feelings once she got to the fair:

> We had a verey good day alltogether, but to tell the truth I did not have any real enjoyment. The thoughts that we had run away from

home unknown to our parents spoiled all my pleasure . . . I tried to enjoy myself but I knew the next day I had to leave home and friends and I did not like the idea of my father and mother being angrey with me before I left home. My last day home I thought many times through the day I wished I had staid home with them for the last day.

Lois and Patience ended up spending the night with an aunt and returning home the next day. They received the scolding they expected. The moment was especially painful for everyone because of Patience's impending departure. She did not know when she would be returning. She bid a tearful goodbye to her family and clung to her father's promise to visit her frequently.

Patience's job at the boarding school was an experience in very hard work, long hours, low pay (two pounds ten shillings, about $12.50, a year), and pangs of homesickness. When she was led to her room at the school and saw the scant furniture and small bed, she realized that in all her seventeen years she had never slept by herself in a bed before. "The verey idea of sleeping in a larg old fashoned room all alone made me allmost shuder at the thought, for at home my eldest sister and I had a room to ourselves and we allways slept together," she wrote.

Soon after Patience's arrival, the mistress of the boarding school explained her duties:

> I would have to rise very early in the morning to sweep and dust the large breakfast room, the hall and door steps, and brighten the door knob and knoker, all before breakfast. . . . There were eight rooms to keep clean and the washing done once a month.

On wash days, the mistress of the school required her to get up at midnight and go out "in the cold and dark" to the washhouse in back of the school. There she built a fire to heat the wash water. By 6:00 A.M., the water was hot enough and the scrubbing commenced—and continued for three full days. Washing clothes once a month for nine people besides herself proved to be quite a task for Patience.

The cold, damp English climate caused Patience to suffer miserably from chilblains, a swelling of the hands and feet caused by exposure. But she received little sympathy from her employer and was forced to keep up her heavy work schedule. She longed for home:

When a child I [was] allways troubled with chilblains if I was exposed to cold. But then I had a good kind mother to attend to me and rap up my feet warm. But . . . I left home . . . and no good kind mother to doctor me and let me rest from work. . . . I realy did find there was no place like home.

Patience's life took on a broader and more exciting perspective the day she boarded a coach for London and found employment there. She was thrilled to see places she had heard about all her life. She attended the theater, went to the world-famous Zoological Gardens in Regents Park, picnicked at Greenwich, and strolled past Parliament and other large palaces and government buildings, including Whitehall. She and her girlfriends frequently went to the huge parks where bands played and where they could rent ponies from "gypsies" (for sixpence an hour) and enjoy an afternoon of horseback riding. During her stay in London, she witnessed the funeral procession of the Duke of Wellington, which she described as "a grand sight" as it wound its way to St. Paul's Cathedral.

For any country girl, life in London would have been quite an adventure; for Patience, whose upbringing was especially strict and protected, it was bliss. Her employers were generally very kind and allowed her time to socialize. But their religious convictions caused them to caution her about attending the theater "too frequently."

Patience had worked away from home six years when she heard reports that her parents had joined the Mormon church. She was sure this was not so, but wrote home just to clear up the misunderstanding. To her great surprise, a letter from her parents confirmed that the reports were true. They had indeed been baptized by missionaries and now called themselves "Latter-day Saints." Patience quickly wrote back, saying she was shocked at their "conceit" in calling themselves "saints" and that she viewed many of their new beliefs as pure "nonsense."

As Patience made periodic visits home during the next three years, she listened more tolerantly to the teachings of the new church, and she began to like what she heard. One of her objections to her own religious surroundings had been that everyone looked so serious and did not seem to believe in laughing, dancing, or having much fun. She heard the Mormons, however, teach a gospel of happiness, joy, and optimism. This new outlook and the doctrines of the new faith soon began to fill her mind and heart, and it pleased her. During one of her visits home to Oxfordshire, Patience "was led by the Spirit of God to chuse the good part." She was baptized in June 1853 at the age of twenty-six.

Difficult tests of her faith in the restored gospel began almost immediately. At the time of her baptism, Patience was working at the fashionable Burlington Hotel in London; she was quickly fired by the housekeeper, who said, "We don't want no Mormons in this house." Her sister Eliza, living in the same hotel, was so bitter about Patience's baptism that she did not come to say goodbye when Patience packed her things and left.

In spite of this division in the family, the faith of the parents and most of the children grew, and within two years James and Amy Loader, Patience, three sisters, and two brothers were making preparations to emigrate to America to join the Saints in Utah. On December 12, 1855, they sailed from Liverpool with five hundred Danish Saints and a few German, Italian, French, and Scottish families. The emigrants organized themselves and distributed supplies according to need. Elder Canute Peterson was appointed to serve as president over the whole company. Everyone was cheerful and had high hopes for a pleasant voyage.

The crossing of the Atlantic Ocean, however, took considerably longer than expected—eleven weeks in all—and resulted in sixty-two deaths among the passengers. The two lower decks, where the sleeping berths were located, were dark, poorly ventilated, and dirty. Patience wrote of her first night aboard the ship when she could not find a berth to sleep in:

> I began to think we would smother to death before morning, for there was not a breath of air. I made my bed on a large box. I had a big loaf of bread in a sack. This I used for my pillow to make sure of having bread for breakfast. This was not a verey nice thing to do—to sleep on my bread.

They encountered a series of storms along the way and many suffered miserably from seasickness as well as from malnutrition and pneumonia. Patience described the losses endured by the Loader family and others on the ship:

> My brother buried his little girl Zilpha. It did indeed seem very hard to roll her in a blanket and lay her in the big waves and see the little dear go floting away out of sight. There was one Danish brother and sister—their two sons, all the children they had, boath died and was

buried in the sea. The eldest was eleven years old and the younger nine
I think. This was very severe trial for this poor brother and sister. They
was faithfull good Latter-day Saints and they was welthey people and
had been the means of several poor familys coming to Utah. But the
loss of their two only children seemed allmost more than thay could
endure.

In spite of the poor conditions aboard the ship and the language
barrier between those from different countries, the Saints enjoyed
each other's company. Several of the Danish Saints brought musical
instruments, and so, among other amusements, dances were held
regularly. Patience and her sisters were popular dance partners. But
even such merriment eventually wore thin, and the Saints "grew
tired and worn out" as the weeks passed with no sign of land.

During a storm one night, when the Loader family had nearly
lost hope of arriving safely in America, Patience recorded:

> Just when the ship was tosing and rolling the worst I opened my
> eyes. We was all in darkness. But in a moment the curtain [to her
> sleeping berth] opened and a beautifull lovely figure stood there. Oh
> such a lovely countenance I had never seen before in all my life, and the
> light was so bright around him that I could see the colour of his eyes
> and hair. He had brown eyes and lovely brown hair, and he spoke to
> me as I looked at him. He sais "Fear not, you shall be taken there all
> safe." Then he left and the curtens was again closed.

The voyage was eventually completed, and tears of joy were shed
in February of 1856 when land was sighted and the ship docked at
Castle Gardens, now Ellis Island. The Loaders quickly set about
finding a place to live temporarily in New York City. They planned
to stay there for a year to earn enough money to outfit themselves
for the trek west. In May, however, they received word from Elder
Franklin D. Richards, president of the European Mission, that they
should leave immediately for Iowa City and prepare to travel west
by handcart that summer. "This was a terrable great suprise to us
all," wrote Patience. "At first we fealt we never could undertake to
pull a hancart from Iowa to Salt Lake City and my poor mother in
delicate health. She had not walked a mile for years and we girls had
never been used to outdoor work."

For Patience, the counsel was doubly difficult:

> I think I fealt the worst out of all the family. I could not see it right at
> all to want us to do such a humeliating thing. To be . . . harnest up like

cattle and pull a handcart loded up with our beding, cooking utensils, and our food and clothing, and have to go through different towns to be looked at and made fun of as I knew we would be. It was very hurtfull to my feelings; yes, I will say to my pride.

When the Loaders and other immigrants arrived in Iowa City, little was ready for them. They had to wait most of July while their handcarts were constructed, and consequently they reached Council Bluffs three weeks behind schedule. The group was divided into two companies, the Loaders being assigned to the one led by Edward Martin. James Willie served as captain of the other company.

Even though they realized that in starting so late in the season they risked an encounter with early winter storms, the two groups nonetheless voted to leave right away for the Salt Lake Valley. That decision dealt the Martin and Willie handcart companies "the worst disaster in the history of Western migration."

Once out on the trail, carts broke down, cattle stampeded, and provisions ran out. One hundred miles into their journey, Patience described their plight:

> My father and myself use to be on the inside of the shafts of the cart and my sisters Maria and Jane pulled with a rope tied to the shafts, and Sarah pushed behind. That afternoon we had not traveled far when my poor sick father fell down and we had to stop to get him up on his feet. I said father you are not able to pull the cart. You had better not try to pull. We girls can do it this afternoon. Oh he said, . . . I must not give up. . . . I want to go to the valley to shake hands with Brigham Young.

James Loader grew weaker and weaker, and soon had to let his teenage daughters take over pulling the cart. When they got to camp that night, Patience's sister Zilpha gave birth to a baby boy, and her sister Tamar came down with Rocky Mountain spotted fever. This forced them to remain behind the rest of the company, maintaining all-night fires to keep away marauding wolves. They eventually caught up with their company, but inclement weather and lack of provisions soon took their toll. James Loader died on the trail on September 24. Patience wrote:

> We had to rap my dear father in a quilt, all we had to rap him in. No nice casket to lay him away in comfortable, but put into the grave and the earth thrown in upon his poor body. Oh that sounded so hard I will

never forget the sound of that dirt being shoveld onto my poor father's body. It seemed to me that it would break every bone in his body. It did indeed seem a great trial to have to leave our dear father behind that morning, knowing we had looked upon that sweet smiling face for the last time on earth; but not without a hope of meeting him again in the morning of the resurrection.

Before the companies were out of the Black Hills of Wyoming, and a full month before snow usually fell, the most violent winter to hit the region in many years descended upon them. Many nights, after the company had crossed a river or stream, Patience and her family had to sleep in muddy, wet, or frozen clothes. The ground was often too solidly frozen to drive in their tent pegs. At one point, the man driving a wagon carrying sick and invalid pioneers missed the trail and became lost. Several men were sent back to find them and they returned that evening, bringing in the nineteen Saints who had been in the wagon—all dead from exposure.

Patience and her sisters gathered wood each evening to make a fire, sometimes trudging through waist-deep snow for a single log. One evening they made broth for supper from boiling an old beef head:

> We got of[f] the skin from the beef head, chopt it in pieces the best I could, put it into the pot with some snow, and boiled for a long time. About four o'clock in the afternoon we was able to have some of this fine made broath. I cannot say it tasted very good, but it was flavord boath with sagebrush and from the smokey fire from the green ceder fire. So after it was cooked we all enjoyed it and fealt very thankfull to have that much.

By the time the company had gotten as far as the Platte River, they were in a deplorable condition. They were still 700 miles from the Salt Lake Valley, and their rations, which had been reduced to four ounces of flour per person, would last only another eight to ten days. Some had little clothing and were walking in deep snow barefoot or with tattered rags around their feet, leaving a trail of blood. Some mornings they arose to find that as many as twenty members of their company had died during the night.

On October 4, President Brigham Young received word that the two handcart companies, more than 1,200 souls, were still on the trail. President Young immediately called for volunteers to launch a massive rescue effort. Wagons were quickly loaded with clothes, food, and other supplies. Many anxious relatives volunteered to go to the aid of their loved ones.

It was October 28 before the scouts for the rescue party found the Martin Company. Dan Jones describes finding the beleaguered handcart company struggling up "a long muddy hill":

> A condition of distress here met my eyes that I never saw before or since. The train was strung out for three or four miles. There were old men pulling and tugging their carts, sometimes loaded with a sick wife or children—women pulling along sick husbands—little children six to eight years old struggling through the mud and snow. As night came on the mud would freeze on their clothes and feet.

Many of the sturdy volunteers broke down and wept when they saw the suffering of these Saints. Robert Burton's account book shows that the following supplies were disbursed to aid the immigrants: 102 pairs of boots and shoes, 157 pairs of socks and stockings, 30 quilts and comforters, 100 frock coats and jackets of various kinds, 36 hoods, 80 petticoats and bloomers, 27 handkerchiefs, 14 neckties, and 8 pairs of mittens. Still, only one of every two persons in the Martin Company now possessed a good coat or a pair of stockings without holes, and each tent shared but one good blanket. In the ensuing days 4,120 pounds of flour and two bushels of onions were distributed. The rescuers also provided wagons for the sick to ride in, and much-needed manpower to gather fuel and build fires, especially for those families who had lost husbands and fathers.

The rescue effort saved most of the handcart pioneers, but death continued to take its toll, including the two-year-old daughter of Patience's sister, Zilpha Jaques. In all, more than 150 members of the Martin Handcart Company, fully one-fourth of the total number, had died by journey's end.

When the company wearily entered the Salt Lake Valley on November 30, Patience was so depressed that she wondered whether it was all worthwhile. After all, the Salt Lake City of 1856 was not London. She wrote:

> When first we arrived in the city, to us everything looked dreary and cold. The streets was all covered with snow, . . . the houses was scattering. To me it seemed a very lonesome place. . . . I had been

living eleven years in the city of London before I left England and to me it seemed a very loanly place. I said to my old friend Annie Thorn, if this is Salt Lake City, what must it be like in the country.

But her attitude quickly changed when she and others in her company were warmly greeted and welcomed into the homes of the Saints. Part of the Loader family went south to Pleasant Grove, Utah, some went north to Farmington, and Patience stayed in Salt Lake City visiting friends from England.

It was two years later, when Patience was thirty-one, that she met John Rozsa, her future husband. The surprising thing in their courtship was that John went to Utah as a soldier in "Johnston's Army." The army had been sent to Utah by President James Buchanan to establish sovereignty over the Mormons, who were falsely reported to be in rebellion against the United States government. Although the so-called Utah War that followed ended without bloodshed, hard feelings and mistrust between the settlers and the soldiers remained for many months. In spite of this tension in the community, Patience and John met, courted, and finally were married in December 1858 in Lehi, Utah. John had been baptized a member of the Church just a few days before their wedding and he proved to be "a most devoted husband and father."

Even with this happy marriage, Patience's sorrows were not over. In 1861 the Civil War broke out, and John was called to Washington, D.C., to fight on the Union side. Patience went with him, their first child in her arms, and lived in uncomfortable and sometimes dangerous circumstances until John was discharged five years later.

John survived many dangerous battles, but was severely weakened by his service in the war. On their way back to Utah in 1866, John died on May 25 and was buried on the plains. Patience was grief stricken. She had three small boys to raise, and was pregnant with their fourth child.

The family continued the journey and arrived in Pleasant Grove in July, relieved to be once more near Patience's mother and other members of her family. Two months later, in September, Patience gave birth to a baby girl. The family now numbered four children: John James, Jr., Frank Loader, Joseph William, and the new baby, Amy Rosalie, named after her two grandmothers. Just one month after giving birth to Amy, while Patience was still grieving over the death of her husband, her sorrow was again multiplied with the death of little Frank at the age of four years.

Not broken by her sorrows, Patience courageously raised her remaining three children and worked hard to clothe, feed, and educate them. She also raised another baby girl, whom she named Ruth, who was left on her doorstep in 1901.

Patience's daughter Amy later became the first city treasurer of Pleasant Grove, and she was succeeded in that office by her mother. Patience also served as one of the first Relief Society presidents in Pleasant Grove and became a dearly loved and respected member of the community. She married John B. Archer, also from England, who died in 1909.

Patience was a charming, petite woman. When she went out visiting, she would always wear a long, white apron, a black taffeta coat, black mitts, and a small black hat edged with violets. She was an excellent cook, specializing in gingerbread cookies and "maid-of-honor" jelly-filled cupcakes. Never too old to learn, Patience bought an organ when she was ninety years old and had a friend teach her how to play "Come, Come Ye Saints."

As a reminder of her English background, Patience kept a picture of Queen Victoria displayed prominently on her living room wall. In memory of her gardener-father, she planted her entire yard in tiny violets instead of grass.

In her later years, Patience often invited the girls of the Young Women's Mutual Improvement Association to her home, where she told them the stories of her life in England and her crossing of the Great Plains as a handcart pioneer. She was deeply religious and never regretted the sacrifices she had made for the gospel.

Patience Loader Rozsa Archer died April 22, 1921, at the age of ninety-four. She left a diary in her own handwriting which records the life of one of Mormondom's most remarkable and courageous women.

7

Anna Gaarden Widtsoe
A Life Transformed by a Cobbler's Gift

John A. Widtsoe was twenty-one years old when he graduated with a teaching certificate from a seminarium near the village of Klaebo in central Norway. One of his first teaching assignments was to Fröya, an island in the Norwegian Sea off the west coast of Norway, west of Trondheim Fjord. Fröya was dotted with tiny fishing villages, each with two to a dozen families.

On his first day of school in the village of Titran, the new schoolmaster sat at his desk looking over the classroom full of fisher lads and maidens. His eyes were attracted to a twelve-year-old girl with beautiful brown wavy hair and bright, inquisitive blue eyes who seemed eager to learn. She was Anna Karine Gaarden. Within a week, the schoolmaster recorded in his diary his intentions to marry her when she reached young womanhood.

Anna Gaarden was born June 4, 1849, in the fishing village of Titran, Norway, the eldest of the two daughters of Peder Olsen Gaarden and Beret Martha Haavig. A son had died at birth. Anna's parents were prosperous by modest island standards, her father making a living by piloting foreign ships through the dangerous Norwegian fjords. Daily, at set hours, Peder climbed the highest lookout and scanned the horizon with his spyglasses. If he sighted a ship signalling for "The King Pilot," off he went, good or rough weather, to take charge of the wheel and guide the ship safely to the harbor of its destination. His cordial and social disposition made him popular up and down the coast and placed him in contact with people from many countries.

Because the traffic was heavy past this, the outermost island of Norway, Peder was absent from home much of the time, but his affections were centered around his family and he was proud of his attractive daughters, Anna and Petroline Jorgine.

Anna grew up as a spectator to the magnificent displays of nature Norway presented from season to season. Her home island of Fröya is about thirty-two miles long, the rocky, jagged coast constantly pounded by the foaming waves of the Atlantic Ocean. As spring broke from the long northern winter, Anna thrilled at the wealth and variety of flowers which seemingly grew in every crevice and on every rock. The flowers seemed to compensate for the total lack of trees and shrubbery on the island. Indeed, after Anna immigrated to the United States several years later, she made arrangements to bring bulbs and seeds of some of her favorite flowers from her homeland.

During the summer months, the sun would shine for eighteen to twenty hours each day, and thousands of grey birds came from the south to lay their eggs among the rocky crags. Then in late summer and fall, Anna and Petroline delighted at the onset of the time to harvest berries. Among the rocks and heather, the little girls went with their buckets to pick blueberries, red bitter tytteberries (a relative of the cranberry), and pale yellow multeberries. Anna and her sister had a hard time filling their buckets when eating was so delicious. After a long day, the girls and other little friends would return home with blue-stained fingers and lips but smiling broadly with their buckets full of berries. During the next few days, the fruit was made into mush or preserves. It was an occasion they looked forward to all year.

The beautiful flowers lasted well into the fall season, with new blossoms appearing as others faded. But the winter months were less cheerful as the flowers faded, the birds began their journey south, and the ocean grew more restless and stormy. During the winter, when there were only four or five hours of daylight, the Gaarden family busied themselves at home with various indoor projects. Anna and her sister and mother carded wool they had clipped from their sheep the previous spring, they spun wool thread, and their mother instructed them in the fine art of weaving. Anna especially enjoyed splashing and boiling the white wool in a muddy liquor to have it come out beautifully red, blue, or yellow.

Their tiny island became isolated from the mainland and from other countries during the winter, for few vessels dared to brave the rough waters in the narrow straits. The great ocean was both loved and feared by those who made their living fishing from it. Some-times a windstorm came up quickly while hundreds of men were fishing many miles from shore. The ocean would grow rougher as the men cut loose their nets and tried frantically to get safely back to shore. But often before the waters were calm again, bodies of loved ones were washing up on shore. At one time or another every family on the island lost a father, son, brother, or sweetheart at sea. No family was spared.

As Anna approached the age of ten, a glorious new adventure opened up to her. Her father began taking her with him on his trips to the mainland. She especially enjoyed her visits to Kristiansund ("a town with real streets") and to Trondheim, the ancient Norwegian capital. The age-old cathedral there, it seemed to her, was big enough to hold all the thousands of fishermen who came to Titran at herring time.

When Peder was unable to take Anna with him, he faithfully returned with a gift for her and her sister: a gem from Italy, a bit of lace from France, or a dress pattern from England. The anticipation they felt as they saw his boat land at the shore near their home from such trips was almost too much for the girls to endure.

As a young girl, Anna was taught many skills for running a household as well as some which brought extra income to the family. Anna and Petroline gathered boatloads of seaweed growing near the shore, dried it, and then gently burned the seaweed. The resulting ash was then sent to England, where iodine was extracted from it. In late fall, the girls combined the accumulated fat from the household and the fat livers from small fish, boiling them in great kettles to purify them. Long strips of wick were then dipped into the fat to make candles, or the tallow was poured into molds, a wick in the center of each. Anna pleaded for permission to make baby candles and Christmas candles, a privilege the older folk were not allowed. So, a huge heap of newly-made candles was piled neatly upon the shelf of the Gaarden storehouse for use during the long winter nights.

The fat left over from candlemaking was mixed with alkali, and Anna helped in forming this mixture into soap for use in their home. She and Petroline were firmly warned not to tamper with the hot soap, but they were later allowed to cut the warm soap into figures of men, cows, and horses.

Anna's parents were careful to instruct their daughters in matters of religion as well as temporal skills. One or two Sundays each month, if the sea was quiet, the family attended church on the neighboring island of Hitra, several hours away by boat. The day before, food was prepared, and they were off early Sunday morning, singing as they rowed. The church service was followed by lunch and an hour or two of socializing with friends, and then the trip home. When the weather was foul, making it too dangerous to row to church, family services were held at home, with Anna's father conducting. Anna always felt that their worship services at home were at least as good as those they attended at church.

A custom that stimulated Anna's mind to good thoughts and nourished her intellect took place each evening after the day's work was over. The family, as well as several neighbors, gathered in the large dining-living room of the Gaarden home. The "home evening" began with the singing of a hymn, usually from a collection of songs written nearly two hundred years earlier by Norwegian fisherman-preacher-poet Peder Dass. A chapter of the Bible was read, then Anna's mother or others recited poems or tales from the rich legendary history of Norway. Selections were often played on the flute, violin, or guitar, and then everyone quietly dispersed for the night's rest.

As Anna entered adolescence she found herself hungering for more knowledge, more truth, more progress. She sat up late through the long sunlit summer nights, reading sagas of the north, poetry, and prose. Her sound judgment and often prankish ways made her a leader among her peers. Anna had been an individualist from childhood. She knew her own mind and made her own decisions. Such independence would come to Anna's aid as events in her life would force her to be self-reliant.

Anna's thirst for knowledge and willingness to work for what she wanted made her an excellent student, and the new teacher from Klaebo, John A. Widtsoe, took delight in teaching and training her. For four or five years John gave her semi-private instruction in language, literature, history, and geography. He must have enjoyed the years of educating the mind of the girl he hoped some day to marry.

Just before Anna's twelfth birthday a tremendous blow fell upon the Gaarden family when their dear mother and wife, Beret, died at the age of thirty-two. It was a great shock to the two girls, who adored their mother, and to their father, who was broken-hearted. Anna became her father's confidante and companion. She went on trips with her father more frequently and bore heavy responsibilities with the day-to-day housekeeping tasks as well as the raising of her younger sister, Petroline.

Anna was becoming a young woman, and word of her beauty, vivacity, and intelligence had spread beyond the island. Suitors came from far and near. When she was eighteen the schoolmaster finally told her of his love, which he had harbored for six years. They became engaged when Anna was eighteen, but three years would pass before their marriage. That time allowed John to return to the mainland to receive two additional years of schooling in order to obtain more advanced certification for teaching. Anna and John were married December 29, 1870, in Dolm Church on the island of Hitra, the church at which Anna had worshipped throughout her young life.

The next eight years were termed the "happy years." John continued to teach in Titran and contributed greatly to the community. He allowed the villagers access to his private library, held weekly lectures on various subjects for the public to attend, and read classic prose and poetry at various gatherings for all to hear and appreciate. He conceived the idea of constructing a large assembly hall to be used during the week for lectures and study groups and for religious services on Sunday. The idea caught fire and the community worked together to make the dream a reality. The hall still stands today, a monument to the successful idealism of a young man who set out to help his fellowman.

After Anna's father died in 1871, Anna and John felt less obligated to remain on the island. Both wanted to try their wings on the mainland. John accepted a position in Namsos, a small town north of Trondheim, and Anna was thrilled to explore a new world. By this time their first child, John Andreas Widtsoe, had arrived; five years later, after they had moved to Namsos, a second son was born and given the name of Osborne Johannes Peder Widtsoe.

Anna lived a full and new life in Namsos, attending social gatherings, theater productions, and dances. She also read a lot, especially taking time to study the Bible carefully, comparing its doctrines with those of the churches of the land. All in all, the little family was happy and the future looked promising—but tragedy suddenly came and the "happy years" were over.

Early in February of 1878, when baby Osborne was less than two months old, John Widtsoe, the schoolmaster, was taken ill in the classroom and died three days later. His oldest son would write: "For Anna, the heavens and the earth had been swallowed up in darkness. The story of the weeks that followed would best be left untold. Her faithful sister Petroline came to Namsos by the first boat, and nursed both sister and baby."

At her husband's death, Anna not only was thrown into the depths of grief, but she also wrestled with many spiritual problems: "Was God kind and just? If so, why did he take away my husband? What is the meaning and purpose of life?" Earnestly she prayed and studied to know the will of the Lord, yearning to understand God and his prophets. Her sorrow caused her to dig deep for answers, many of which were soon to come in a way she never would have expected. It began with a trip to the shoemaker.

Anna moved to Trondheim with her two boys in the hope of finding work there as a dressmaker. Asking a neighbor to recommend a good cobbler to repair her son's shoes, she was told that Olaus Johnsen was very competent. Upon arriving at his shop and giving him the shoes that required new soles, she turned to leave when the shoemaker said, somewhat hesitantly, "You may be surprised to hear me say that I can give you something of more value than soles for your child's shoes." Anna, surprised, turned and asked, "What can you, a shoemaker, give me better than soles for my son's shoes? You speak in riddles." The cobbler then bore his testimony of the latter-day gospel, saying it contained the Lord's true plan of salvation as Anna had never heard it before. Anna left the shop skeptical but with the man's words still ringing in her ears. When the repaired shoes were brought to her home two days later, Anna found carefully tucked into each shoe some Mormon tracts.

Anna studied and prayed and attended Mormon meetings in Trondheim for the next two years, before becoming convinced that she had found the truth she had been searching for. She was baptized April 1, 1881, by Elder Anthon L. Skanchy in the icy waters of a fjord on the edge of Trondheim.

Anna was the only member of her family to join the Church, although her sister Petroline was baptized several years later after Anna had immigrated to Utah. To her great sorrow, her own family as well as her husband's relatives would have nothing more to do with her after hearing of her baptism. Those who had fed, clothed, and nursed her through her childhood and recent widowhood now preferred not to speak to her. Heavyhearted but more determined than ever to keep the commandments of the Lord, Anna decided to join her newly acquired family of fellow Saints in Utah and made plans to immigrate to America. When John was eleven and Osborne five, Anna joined a party of other Saints from Norway, Denmark, Sweden, and England and embarked on the *S. S. Wisconsin* for New York City.

Anna settled with her two sons in Logan, Utah. The adjustment was not an easy one, especially because of the language barrier, but Anna set about making her home a place of comfort and beauty. Just before her sister Petroline left Norway to join her in Logan, Anna wrote her the following note:

> In this letter I send you five dollars, which use as you desire, but . . . if you can, buy and bring with you . . . two myrtles with strong roots, several bulbs of Mrs. Rian's white lilies, as many bulbs as you can secure of Jacob's lilies, and as many rare flowers as you can conveniently secure. Place them in a tight cigar box containing right good garden soil. Water them carefully along the way.

She then added rather sarcastically: "I hope this box will not give you any more trouble than John and Osborne caused me."

Anna, who became a diligent genealogist, was thrilled when the Logan Temple was finished, providing her the opportunity to do temple work for her father, mother, husband, and other deceased relatives. The spiritual enrichment she received the day in 1884 when she attended the dedication of the Logan Temple was ample reward for whatever sacrifices she had made for the gospel. Her son John wrote, "It seemed to her as if the heavens had opened and the very voice of God had been heard by her. She had never been so near the heavenly hosts before. The same spirit was upon her when she received her own endowments on April 15, 1887."

Anna supported her family by dressmaking, at one time organizing and teaching a sewing school in downtown Logan. When they became old enough, Anna's sons also worked to help support the family and pay for extra lessons and schooling. Anna was eager for John and Osborne to obtain an excellent education as well as cultural training. She saw to it that they had music and art lessons and that they were tutored in English, mathematics, and languages.

John eventually graduated from Brigham Young College in Logan and then went to Harvard, where he graduated with high honors. He later served as president of both Utah State Agricultural College (now Utah State University) in Logan and the University of Utah in Salt Lake City. He became an Apostle of the Church in 1921. Osborne was the valedictorian of his graduating class from Utah State Agricultural College and also graduated from Harvard. He later became president of the Latter-day Saints University in Salt Lake City and head of the English department at the University of Utah. Both John and Osborne served the Church as members of the general board of the Young Men's Mutual Improvement Association.

Anna's sister, Petroline, never married, becoming a lifelong companion for Anna in Logan and later in Salt Lake City. A dream came true for both of them in 1903 when they received mission calls to preach the gospel in their old homeland, Norway. For the next four and a half years the sisters traveled throughout Norway, giving lectures on Mormon women, strengthening the branches, and trying to correct the many falsehoods and prejudices that had been spread about Mormonism. They were among the first regular women missionaries to serve in Norway. Before returning home at the end of their mission Anna journeyed to Namsos, where she visited old friends, saw the school where her husband had taught, and went to the cemetery to stand by the grave of her husband, the schoolmaster. "Memories of the past filled my heart and overflowed," she wrote in her journal.

Anna returned to Utah, where she remained active in the women's Relief Society organization, the Utah Women's Press Club (a group of Utah women writers, wherein she served one term as president), and various civic affairs. She continued to read avidly, nurtured a beautiful flower garden, and gained satisfaction from her sons' educational and religious achievements.

Anna Karine Gaarden Widtsoe died July 11, 1919, at age seventy, in Salt Lake City. Around her bedside were all the members of her family, including Petroline, her devoted, faithful companion.

Her older son, John, made the following entry in his diary following his mother's funeral: "She was a most devoted mother, loyal to the last degree. Her devotion to the cause of truth was almost sublime. She was self-sacrificing beyond expression in behalf of her own and those who needed help. The great issues of her life always swept before her. To her I owe my inspiration."

8

Minnie Petersen Brown
The Years in "Little Denmark"

Bherhammine (Minnie) Caroline Petersen was only ten months old when her family boarded the sailing vessel *Kenilworth* in 1866 and began their voyage to the United States of America. Her parents, Andrew Petersen and Caroline Dortha Dablistine, had accepted the restored gospel five years earlier in Fredericia, Denmark, and were now eager to take their family of four small children to join the Latter-day Saints in Salt Lake City.

After landing in New York City with 684 other Scandinavian Saints, who had traveled under the direction of Samuel Sprague, the Petersens immediately made preparations to move westward. They joined Joseph S. Rawlins's ox team company of over four hundred people and traveled to Council Bluffs, Iowa, by train and boat. Minnie's mother occasionally let her young daughter walk on the ground so Minnie could later say she had walked on the plains as a tot.

Minnie's family was able to make the trip only through the financial assistance of the Perpetual Emigration Fund, a plan by which Church members already settled in Utah could donate money and goods to aid immigrants in coming to the Great Basin. Some families were able to pay their own way but used Church-chartered ships and organizational facilities; others needed partial assistance; and a third group had to rely completely on Church funds.

Andrew and Caroline Petersen had saved enough to pay their expenses in crossing the ocean, but the Church provided the money they needed to cross the Plains to Salt Lake City. As with the other families, they were expected to reimburse the Church either by working on Church projects or donating their surplus produce or cash. Minnie remembers her father saying years later, "Well, that is the last immigration payment and we are happy." By 1870, the Perpetual Emigration Fund had assisted more than 13,000 Saints to immigrate from Scandinavian and European countries and more than 38,000 from the British Isles.

The Petersens arrived in Salt Lake City in October of 1866, just three months after Minnie's first birthday. But their travels were far from over. Nearly every pioneer family moved their place of residence every two or three years. Before Minnie was married at the age of eighteen, the Petersens would move twelve times to various locations in the Salt Lake Valley and in Summit County in eastern Utah. Most of these moves were intended to put her father closer to available work, since commuting long distances was very difficult. At one point they lived in a dugout in the Thirty-third South area of Salt Lake City; one of her younger brothers, Andrew, was born there.

Life for a pioneer girl growing up in Kamas Valley, also known as "Little Denmark," was one of hard work. From an early age Minnie helped tend the garden, care for the chickens, calves, and lambs, helped milk the family's twenty cows, and did a lot of washing, ironing, and cooking. But young Minnie's memories were sweetened by an "angel mother" who made life enjoyable even when there was a task to be done:

> Mother went walking with us on the hillside gathering wild flowers, and also to the meadows where we found shady places beneath the trees to eat the lunch she had prepared. She liked picnics and often told us stories of her childhood days when she lived with her parents on the banks of a river. We gathered wild strawberries, currants and gooseberries which grew along the streams. Mother made a pudding from the juice of these fruits which was very nice. It tasted a good deal like the jello we have today.

Partly because of the frequent moves, partly because of poverty, most girls received very little education. Here again, her mother made Minnie's life an exception. "My mother taught her children to read, write and figure. She felt so bad to think her children could not have an education as she received in the old country (Denmark). To teach us geography she made an outline map with small streams of water, islands, lakes, peninsulas, and continents. To teach arithmetic she had us count doughnuts or clay marbles.''

Even as a young child, Minnie was expected to do various jobs in the yard and around the house, and to run errands for her parents and neighbors. She was once asked to weed a neighbor's flower bed. Not receiving proper instruction, she simply went out and pulled up all the plants that didn't have blossoms on them. ''What a scolding I got,'' she later remembered. On another occasion, her father sent her over to Brother Olsen, the blacksmith, to borrow a monkey wrench. To help her remember the name of the tool, her father told her to think of a little animal. When Minnie asked for the wrench, she asked for a mouse wrench. From that time on, she was known as Mouse Wrench Minnie.

But many of her work experiences were combined with enjoyable social contacts with other young people. As a teenager, she and several of her friends were instructed to clear some land for cultivation. They chopped down willows and sagebrush, picked up rocks and hauled them off, and in the evening had a big bonfire of all the brush. All the young people in the village were there. They roasted potatoes to eat with salt and hung pieces of fresh meat over the fire. They played games and exchanged ghost stories. They combined the picking of fruits and berries with swimming in the creeks. In most groups there was nearly always one person who played the concertina, harmonica, or violin, and so they often had accompaniment for group singing and dancing. They also enjoyed candy pulls and sleigh-riding in the wintertime.

Pioneer life was full of close encounters with death, and Minnie had several such experiences. She once became frightened upon seeing Indians coming while she was gathering eggs in the haystack. She fell between two huge stacks of hay, and would have smothered if her brother Fred hadn't come along and pulled her out. When she was ten, she met a herd of Texas steers while running an errand and was nearly gored to death before a ranch hand rode up and pulled her onto his horse. When she was twelve, she was left alone tending several small children. A whirlwind suddenly came up and she ran for the children and took them down into the cellar. Minnie remembered, ''The roof blew off the house, dishes were broken, and other damage done. Brother Fred was coming home on a horse and when he saw what was happening he drove fast to save us. Father and Mother praised me for running to the cellar with the children."

By the time Minnie was fifteen, she began to have a desire to have nicer clothes than her parents could afford for her. "Some of the young men were becoming interested—well, that was enough—I must have new dresses," she wrote. With her parents' permission, Minnie left the family home in Kamas Valley and hired out, working at an inn in Echo, Utah, cooking, waiting on tables, and helping mothers with new babies. She was paid an average of $2.50 a week and worked from twelve to fourteen hours a day. Although the hours were long, there were always lots of parties and dances to attend and Minnie even learned to roller skate.

Minnie describes meeting her future husband: "I hadn't been in Echo long before I met some very nice boys. They all treated me with respect. I became engaged to a Mr. Jones and everything was going fine until George Brown came to town. I talked with Mr. Brown whenever we met, but in the opinion of Mr. Jones it was too often. So, Mr. Jones and I had a little talk about Mr. Brown and our engagement was broken. . . . Mr. Brown and I soon became sweethearts, then engaged, and began making our plans for marriage."

Minnie Petersen and George Brown were married July 31, 1884 in the Salt Lake Endowment House and were immediately called, along with one hundred other families, to settle in Arizona. The following spring they settled in St. John's, Arizona, where their first child, a son, was born. Two years later, they were released from their mission and returned to Utah to raise a family of six children in Coalville. Widowed at the age of forty-five, Minnie provided for her family by sewing, boarding miners, and leasing the Cluff Hotel in Summit Valley. She worked for the Red Cross and was captain of the Coalville Camp of the Daughters of Utah Pioneers. She was loved and respected by all who came in contact with her and was lovingly called "Aunt Minnie" or "Grandma Brown." A tribute written for her shortly before her death included the following:

> Pioneer Brown is a lovely lady, benevolent and trustworthy, who through the years has learned how to grow old gracefully. Today, in her ninetieth year, she takes care of her home, makes her own clothing and still lends a willing hand to all those who need her. May her remaining years be filled with peace and happiness.

9

Susanna Goudin Cardon

From the Italian Alps to the Rockies

Susanna Goudin was born July 30, 1833 in Prarustin, Piedmont, in Northern Italy, to Barthelemi Goudin and Marthe Cardon. They were one of several thousand transplanted French families who had been forced to take refuge in the remote Alpine mountains because of severe religious persecutions. To understand Susanna and the environment she grew up in, one must become acquainted with the fascinating story of her ancestors, the Waldensians.

The Waldensians (*Valdese* in Italian; *Vaudois* in French) were a Protestant group whose unique religious beliefs had caused hatred among outsiders for many centuries. They claimed an unbroken succession of pastors back to the original Apostles of Christ, considering themselves the oldest continuous Protestant community in the world. One scholar has referred to them as the "Israel of the Alps." They believed that oaths even in a court of justice were not allowable, that homicide was under no circumstances justifiable, that every lie was a mortal sin, that all believers were capable of priestly functions, and that the sacraments were invalidated by uncleanliness of life in the officiating priest.

Later, the group came to repudiate the invocation of the Virgin and saints, and the concept of purgatory. They also made no distinction between laity and priesthood. The group sought a simpler practice of Christian ideals and renounced what they considered Catholic pomp and piety.

Because of their refusal to submit to the power of Rome, the Waldensians were hated and despised by popes and monarchs for centuries. Hardly a generation escaped the torture and bloodshed inflicted upon them because they were considered "teachers of dangerous doctrine." They were burned at the stake, buried alive, hanged, herded into vile and disease-laden dungeons, and hunted down by bloodhounds, pursued from glen to glen, over rocks and crags and icy mountains. Yet the Waldenses defied their assailants and maintained their ancient faith.

The Goudins and other Waldensian families lived pure and simple lives. The families participated in Bible reading, and parents taught their children the ways of their ancient faith during daily religious study in the home.

As more and more fled to the Piedmont at the foot of the Italian Alps, the area became overcrowded and they were reduced to living as peasants and shepherds. The terrain of the valleys was rugged, narrow, and steep—barely wide enough to cultivate food or to graze a few animals. They lived on chestnuts, grapes, figs, and the products of the few sheep and goats they could raise.

Because of the steep terrain, it was a common sight to see people, even aged women, traveling up steep mountain trails with baskets of soil on their backs to replace, each year, the soil that had washed down the steep slopes. Descendants today, upon visiting the land of their ancestors, have expressed surprise that any people could eke out a living from the limited areas to which the Waldenses were confined. The mountainsides still contain no roads—not even pathways wide enough for a donkey to travel. Only on foot can one follow the narrow winding paths that rise up thousands of feet within a short climb into the cloudy mists.

Such was the environment into which Susanna Goudin was born. Her father died when Susanna was just five years old, leaving his wife and four young children to struggle and scrape for a livelihood. At this early age, Susanna had to work and help support the family. She picked potatoes, gleaned the fields, and gathered sticks to be used in the vineyard.

Susanna was only nine years old when she had to leave her poverty-stricken mother and brother and sisters in their mountain home to work to support herself. She earned ten cents a day at this age by picking mulberry leaves to feed silkworms. Later, at the age of twelve, she learned to reel silk and earned twenty cents per day.

When Susanna was fifteen, the king of Sardinia, who ruled the Piedmont, issued a proclamation that would change the course of her life and the lives of a handful of other families who had taken refuge there. On February 17, 1848, the royal monarch granted religious, civil, and political rights to the Waldenses. The very next year, Mormon Apostle Lorenzo Snow was called to open a mission in Italy. Elder Snow was in England at the time, and wrote in his autobiography:

> As I contemplate the condition of Italy with deep solicitude to know the mind of the Spirit as to where I should commence my labors, I found that all was dark in Sicily, the hostile laws would exclude our efforts. No opening appeared in the cities of Italy; but the history of the Waldenses attracted my attention. Amid the ages of darkness and cruelty, they had stood immovable almost as the wave-beaten rock in the stormy ocean.

Arriving in Genoa on July 1, 1850, Elder Snow sent Elders Joseph Toronto and T. B. H. Stenhouse to visit the Protestant valleys of Piedmont. Three weeks later, in a letter to President Franklin D. Richards of the European Mission, Elder Snow said, "I believe that the Lord has there hidden up a people amid the Alpine mountains, and it is the voice of the Spirit that I shall commence something of importance in that part of this dark nation."

Two months later, the missionaries began actively preaching and many Waldensians were attracted to the restored gospel. In fact, the first and only converts to the gospel in Italy during the nineteenth century were Waldensians—families with names like Goudin, Cardon, Malan, Stalle, Beus, and Chatelaine.

Susanna worked away from home most of her teenage years and was therefore not at home when the missionaries preached the gospel to the rest of her family and baptized them. Hence, she was the last one in her family to be converted. She was baptized by George Dennis Keaton on August 18, 1853, at age twenty, and was confirmed by Jabez Woodward in a mountain village in the Piedmont.

By this time, Church leaders in Salt Lake City had issued an epistle urging all Saints to come to Utah and Susanna was filled with the spirit of gathering. The rest of the family became embittered toward their new faith, however, and in 1855 Susanna said good-bye to them and began her journey to the promised land. She traveled with a group which included the Pierre (Peter) Stalle family, who were distant relatives, but she was the only member of her immediate family to emigrate.

The group traveled by carriage, railway, sled, and foot to France, then by steamer to London, and thence by rail to Liverpool where they remained a short time waiting for a ship. On December 12, 1855, they set sail on the *John J. Boyd* under the supervision of Elder Canute Peterson, arriving in New York three months later on March 15, 1856.

From New York City, the emigrants boarded a train for St. Louis, Missouri, and then proceeded to Florence, Nebraska, which served as a regrouping site for the Saints heading west. The very year the Waldenses arrived there, Church leaders decided to begin trans-porting emigrants by handcart rather than by animal-drawn wagons. The handcarts could carry about one hundred pounds of provisions, served five to six people, and were pulled by the emigrants themselves. Twenty-three-year-old Susanna, the other Waldenses, and a large group of other European Saints would be part of the first handcart company organized by the Church.

During the three-month-long wait during which preparations were being made for the journey, Susanna worked in Florence for a shopkeeper by the name of Samuel Lee. She helped in his home and also helped pick fruit in his orchard. The Lees were good to her and when she left, they gave her a new dress and bonnet. They also gave her a feather tick, but since it was considered a luxury for the journey west she was not allowed to take it with her.

While in Florence, Susanna met and fell in love with a young Englishman who lived there. Though Susanna evidently loved him dearly, he was not a member of the Church and refused to join. Several months later, when the handcart company was ready to pull out, Susanna was faced with the difficult decision of whether to pro-ceed with her fellow Waldensians to the Great Salt Lake Valley or to stay with the Englishman. After much thought and prayer, she decided to go with the Saints, a decision that was not without re-grets, and one that would trouble her for some time.

The handcart company finally departed, with Susanna pulling a handcart most of the 1,400 miles. Crossing the plains under the direction of Edmund Ellsworth, they arrived in Salt Lake City on September 26, 1856. Of the 273 members of that first company leaving Nebraska, 33 gave up the trip before their arrival in the Salt Lake Valley and 12 died along the way.

The challenge of leading a large, diverse, and very inexperienced group of people across the wilderness must have been great for Captain Ellsworth, and the trip was not without tensions and personal conflicts. One interesting coincidence is the fact that the person who was to become Susanna's future husband's second wife, Madelaine Beus, rode most of the way across the plains in Susanna's handcart. Little Madelaine was two years old at the time.

As the company entered the Salt Lake Valley, President Brigham Young and other dignitaries rode out to meet them, presenting them with gifts of Utah-grown melons. A procession was formed and paraded into the city, where the tired pioneers were greeted with cheers and pomp. Susanna's journey from her homeland in Italy had taken nine months.

In spite of the persecutions Susanna had experienced in Italy and the exhausting migration to Utah, these experiences only served to prepare this twenty-three-year-old woman for the difficult life that still lay ahead of her in pioneering a new land.

Fortunately for Susanna, a fellow Waldensian family had arrived in the Salt Lake Valley two years earlier. The Philippe Cardons, who had settled in Ogden, eagerly set out to help the new Italian immigrants when they heard of their arrival. Two of the Cardon sons, Paul and Phillip, immediately went to Salt Lake City and brought the Pierre Stalle family and Susanna back to Brigham's Fort in north Ogden. Margaret Stalle Baker described how the Cardons helped them through the first severe winter: "While in Ogden, they were snowed in their dugout, without matches or a clock. They did not even get out of bed as they could not tell the time or make a fire. Paul Cardon came and dug them out."

Young Paul Cardon became so well acquainted with Susanna that within a short time he proposed marriage. Although he was a handsome, hardworking young man and a devoted member of the Church, Susanna hesitated for several reasons. He was sixteen and she was twenty-three; and they were already first cousins—her mother, Marthe Cardon Goudin, and his father, Philippe Cardon, were brother and sister. The other was her remaining affection for the Englishman she had left behind in Nebraska. Susanna's granddaughter, Rebecca Cardon Hickman Peterson, later observed:

> At this time she was very much in love with the young Englishman but because she was alone and was influenced by Father Cardon, she married him (Paul). She grieved over this for a year. In fact, until she went to the Endowment House. She wept bitterly when she went there. Brigham Young, seeing her, sensed her trouble and told her to go through and all would be well with her. And this was literally fulfilled, as when they were old I have seldom seen a more devoted couple.

They were married March 16, 1857 and eventually had six sons and five daughters. Both contributed greatly to the Church and community.

Susanna and Paul moved further north in Utah to settle in Cache Valley, where she immediately noticed similarities between the climate of that area and the Piedmont valleys in northern Italy. They sent to France for mulberry tree seeds, hoping to establish a home silk industry which Susanna would manage with talents learned as a child in Italy. Brigham Young had lately encouraged the Saints in self-sufficiency and he was more than supportive of any effort to produce silk locally. Eventually the Women's Relief Society organized the Deseret Silk Association, and during the 1870s nearly 150 communities sponsored silk projects. In 1877, producers boasted of five million silkworms and President Young personally directed the transplanting of some one hundred thousand mulberry trees in all parts of Utah to provide leaves necessary to feed the silkworms.

Susanna's unusual skill established her as one of the leaders in this industry. She became heavily involved in teaching inexperienced women how to make silk, a procedure requiring talent and practice because of the delicate way in which the worms manufacture the thread. Each silkworm spins a cocoon about the size of a peanut; this ''peanut'' is actually a continuous silk thread 1,000 to 1,300 yards long. Reeling the silk from this cocoon was a skill in which Susanna excelled. Brigham Young was especially impressed with her abilities:

> As he watched her work he thought she must have some trick in handling the silk threads. So she put her hand in his and took it

through the process giving it a quick flip and putting it on the reel, thus showing that it was all in knowing how to handle it. The silk she wove was of a very high grade and was as good as any from Italy.

Susanna was eventually called by President Young on a three-month silk mission to Salt Lake City. This meant leaving behind eight children, including a year-old baby. Upon her return to Logan, she continued to teach her silk skills to local women through the Relief Society organization. Samples of her silk were shown at various times at county and state fairs and for the excellence of her work she received medals from New Jersey, California, and the World's Fair at Chicago.

Her patience with her pupils bore fruit; in 1876 Utah's exhibit at the centennial of the United States in Philadelphia included silk dresses for which the material had been raised, reeled, woven, and sewn in Utah.

Susanna loved people and they in return loved her. Her faith in the Lord was great and her charity and integrity were known everywhere she went. When asked how she could have raised a large family so well, without having had any education or advantages of any kind, she indicated her reliance on prayer when she replied that she had raised them "on her knees."

She was a loving wife who took pleasure and pride in the well-clothed appearance of her husband and children. She herself was always neat, clean, and well dressed. Descendants remember that she was always busy with some kind of handiwork and many of them have samples of her knitting, crocheting, and silk. One grand-daughter, Margaret Cardon Hickman of Logan, remembered how she loved canaries and always had several which sang beautifully.

In 1892, Susanna and Paul moved to Benson Ward, a small community northwest of Logan, where they farmed for twenty years. But in 1913 they returned to Logan to do temple work and to be closer to their children living there.

The Cardon family today is recognized as one of the prominent families of Utah and Arizona. Susanna and Paul's descendants gradually achieved distinction and eminence. They served their community as politicians, jewelers, investors, teachers, chemists, and restaurateurs, and some began a prominent land-title business. They have served in all organizations of the Church, and several have become bishops, stake presidents, and patriarchs; one son,

Louis Samuel Cardon, served as president of the Swiss Mission. One of Paul and Susanna's granddaughters, Lucile Cardon Reading, served in the general presidency of the Primary and was editor of the *Friend* magazine for twelve years before her death in 1982.

Susanna died at the age of eighty-seven on December 8, 1920, leaving a posterity of eleven children, sixty grandchildren, and forty-five great-grandchildren. She is buried in the Logan Cemetery overlooking Cache Valley, which she and her husband helped to settle.

Part Three

Pioneering
in the West

10

Mary Jane Mount Tanner
Reader, Writer, Teacher

Twelve-year-old Mary Jane Mount pulled the well-worn blanket tighter around her shivering body and inched closer to the warm, crackling fire. Outside the crudely built one-room shelter several miles up Mill Creek Canyon, southeast of Salt Lake City, wild animals howled throughout the night and the wind blew snow drifts against the thin walls.

But inside, Mary Jane's thoughts were far away as she immersed herself in the reading of such classics as Daniel Defoe's *Robinson Crusoe*, Milton's *Paradise Lost*, and Macaulay's *England*, and thoroughly studied the New Testament and the Doctrine and Covenants.

Mary Jane loved books—history, biography, poetry—and as she grew older her love of literature developed into a desire to write and publish her own thoughts and feelings:

> I too have some gems of thought and beautiful ideas that float through my mind like mists on a summer morning. But would they be appreciated? This is such a commonplace world after all, that it would be like putting sugar on our meat and potatoes; it would waste the sugar and spoil the meat. . . . One can say all sorts of things if they are well said, and people are interested and think them witty or smart; but when I have an idea that I consider particularly nice, I turn it over in my mind

until it seems so very stale that if I mention it I expect to hear some one say, "how stupid."

Despite her frustrations, Mary Jane nurtured her desire to write and achieved to some degree her dream of having "a name of note in the literary world."

Mary Jane was born February 27, 1837, the daughter of Joseph Mount and Elizabeth Bessac. Her parents had married in 1832 in Lockport, Niagara County, New York, and moved to Toledo, Ohio, where Mary Jane was born.

Because of her mother's poor health, Mary Jane spent most of her first four years living with her maternal grandparents in New York. Joseph and Elizabeth converted to Mormonism in Dayton, Ohio, and the three joined the Saints gathered in Nauvoo, Illinois, where Joseph made a comfortable life for his family as a reputable wheelright, carpenter, joiner, and millwright.

Mary Jane was ten when severe persecutions made it necessary for the Saints to leave Nauvoo. She watched as her father sold their stove, featherbed, bedding, and some smaller articles in return for a gun and "muley cow." She sensed the fear her parents and the entire community felt as threats were made against their lives. She later recorded her feelings at the beginning of their journey across the plains to the Salt Lake Valley:

> I think I shall never forget that long lonely day; waiting on that vast undulating prairie that stretched as far as the eye could reach, covered with grass and flowers. It must have been a lovely scene that bright spring morning, but I hardly think it was properly appreciated by the little band who were so bravely leaving home, friends, country and kindred to take their toilsome march across the Rocky Mountains. The oxen were detached from the wagons and feeding lazily among the green grass, knowing nothing of the future that lay before them, or that before many months their bones would, many of them, whiten on the desert sands. My childish heart knew as little as they of the hardship that lay before us. My pale delicate mother watched the teams while my father busied himself assisting or counseling those who were starting out. No doubt her heart failed her on that long weary day as she sat in the bright spring sunshine, watching the shadows and thinking of all she was leaving behind, and wondering what the future held in store for her.

Mary Jane admired her sometimes frail mother and marveled at her frequent display of physical strength and endurance during the trek. At one point during the journey, the young boy hired to drive their wagon returned to Winter Quarters, leaving Elizabeth to drive the team:

> Mother drove the team the rest of the way, yoking and unyoking in addition to her other duties. One of her oxen would never learn to hold back, and, when going down hill she had to hold his horn with one hand and pound his nose with the other to keep him from running into the wagon ahead of him. A feat which would astonish some of our belles of the present day, and yet she was reared as tenderly, and as little accustomed to hardship as any of them. Many times the bushes caught her dress and she had no choice but to rush on, leaving it in pieces behind her. . . . I wonder if those coming after knew what those tattered rags meant.

The Mounts, arriving in the Salt Lake Valley in late September, were among the first group to winter there in 1847. It had taken them five months to cover thirteen hundred miles. Mary Jane's first impression was not encouraging; to a young girl who had grown up in New England and the Midwest, the valley "presented a barren aspect . . . covered mostly with sage brush and sunflowers, with a few small streams of water running through it, and some squalid Indian wigwams scattered about." But she and other pioneer children generally cared little about the feasibility of settling an area and were delighted to be living in the "Delectable Mountains."

Mary Jane and her friends enjoyed gathering bouquets of crimson and yellow leaves and a variety of wildflowers while their parents busily prepared shelters for their families before winter set in. Mary Jane's father built a sawpit, sawing logs that others had brought from the canyons. Joseph was so busy sawing logs for others to use for their cabins that it was the middle of December before they moved into their own shelter in the valley. It was built of sawed logs and had a dirt roof. "We had no floor but the ground," Mary Jane wrote, "but we were thankful for a roof. My father laid the floor on Christmas day, and my mother called it a merry Christmas."

When Mary Jane was twelve years old, her father built a sawmill in Mill Creek Canyon and constructed another crude shelter nearby for his family, which had increased in size to four with the birth of a new baby, Cornelia. The eight isolated months the family lived in Mill Creek Canyon were not pleasant ones for a young girl craving social contact. It was during this time that Mary Jane turned more to her books, most of which her father had evidently brought from the Midwest. It was fortunate for Mary Jane that her father was an educated man who appreciated books enough to let them occupy valuable space in the covered wagon on the journey West.

Mary Jane read Parley P. Pratt's *A Voice of Warning* and *The Complete Works of Flavius Josephus* at this time, surprisingly heavy reading for a twelve-year-old.

Aside from the loneliness, the winter months were endlessly cold and windy:

> Our miserable shanty being dark and cold we were glad to keep large fires, logs being put on sometimes which it took two men to lift. We had our yule log for Christmas, but were scant of good cheer. The wind whirled over the mountains and came down [the] chimney, often filling the room with smoke and ashes and frightening us lest the house should catch fire.

Joseph occasionally had to go into the valley to bring back supplies, leaving Mary Jane, her mother, and her baby sister alone for several days in the canyon. Such occasions provided unbearable hardships for the threesome:

> [The mountains] were infested with wild animals whose voices often made night hideous and we often got up in the morning and found the snow nearly to the top of the door and had to dig a way out.

For Mary Jane's mother, the nights were the hardest to endure:

> . . . the thoughts of being entirely alone in that wild place so far from any human habitation, and her cabin so insecurely fastened from wild beasts, gave her feelings she had never before experienced, and we gladly hailed my father's return. He was well pleased to find us safe, for he felt that it was hard to leave us alone.

In the spring of 1849, Mary Jane's father was lured by the prospect of gold in California. He made arrangements for a business partner, a Brother Thompson, to care for his family while he sought his fortune in the gold mines. Mary Jane could hardly blame her father's eagerness to seek financial success elsewhere. "True, the prospects here were very discouraging," she wrote. "Privation and want seemed all that lay before us and it took strong faith or childish simplicity to picture even a comfortable future for Utah."

Her father's partner, however, was careless in his management of the Mounts' daily needs and the family spent several months in living conditions that Elizabeth found unacceptable. Still living in Mill Creek Canyon, they lived on rations of corn meal mush and milk, dried squash, some roots and weeds (such as mustard or pigweed), and a rare loaf of bread.

At Elizabeth's insistence, Brother Thompson finally moved them back into the Salt Lake Valley, at which time their situation improved considerably. The neighbors erected a shelter for them and they purchased a small stove from a friend who had brought it from Green River. After such a long time in the canyon, they were grateful for human companionship, which Mary Jane described ruefully as "acquaintances made in adversity, and friends cemented by common suffering."

Joseph Mount met with some success in California and sent financial support to his family as it became available. Mary Jane was thrilled when they had enough money to buy a dress pattern and her mother promptly colored their wagon-cover and tent and cut them up for wearing apparel. "No city belle was ever prouder of her fine array than I was of my new dress," she bubbled.

During Mary Jane's fourteenth year, her parents had a misunderstanding while her father was still in California which ultimately resulted in a divorce. The event was a crushing blow to Mary Jane and her mother, one that neither of them fully recovered from. The emotional impact of being severed from someone they both still loved was tremendous and once again their economic situation became desperate. Mary Jane described their plight:

> There were funds set apart for the poor and the Church would have provided for [us] a meager subsistence for people were not allowed to starve; but [mother] could not think of living on charity, or drawing supplies from the Church. It was a time of great trials and bitter sorrow, scarcely a ray of hope gilded the pathway. We procured the use of a dilapidated cabin for the summer, and took a sorrowful leave of our home; the first comfortable house we had lived in for many years.

To provide a small bit of income, Mary Jane braided and sold straw hats, her mother took in boarders, and they raised a garden and a few chickens. The family's hopes increased when there was an opening for a schoolteacher in the local ward school. Mary Jane carefully studied her reading, writing, geography, and grammar in the hope of being hired. In spite of her efforts, however, an older woman was considered more qualified by the trustees.

> I returned home mortified and discouraged. I was just beginning my experiences in the world, and every attempt seemed a failure. We wept together, my mother and I, and longed for a strong manly arm to lean upon, the comfort and support of the husband and father. The passing days were fraught with sorrow and disappointments.

A short time after their divorce, Mary Jane's parents each remarried, and neither of the new step-parents was friendly toward sixteen-year-old Mary Jane. Such circumstances left her feeling unwelcome at either home. "Home! Had I a home? The word sounded the least bit dreary sometimes, and if a thought of envy entered my heart it was for those who had fathers and mothers united in a dear home circle."

Mary Jane was religiously inclined and faithfully attended her church meetings. In addition, she had a special zest for dancing, Sunday evening walks, and reading. To forget her "unenviable" family problems, she immersed herself in the "usual rounds" of tea parties, balls, theaters, and mixed social gatherings.

But Mary Jane's earlier years of economic deprivation and poverty made her now more determined than ever to become trained in a vocation that would bring financial security. After passing an examination and receiving her certificate to teach, she found herself behind the teacher's desk of the little schoolhouse of the Salt Lake Eighth Ward.

> My heart swelled as I thought of the responsibility I was taking on myself, but I went forward hopefully, praying God for strength to carry it through. I took an interest in my work for I had a school of bright, interesting pupils. I loved them very much and they returned my kind feelings, bringing flowers and trimming my hair until I must have looked like a miniature flower garden. We were very merry and I found it hard to assume the dignity necessary to my calling.

During her seventeenth year, Mary Jane met Myron Tanner, a young Latter-day Saint from San Bernardino, California, who had come to Utah to sell several horses. Myron's autobiography describes their meeting:

I became acquainted with Jane Mount who was living at the time with Henry Lawrence (a half-brother). Most of my boyhood days my life was separate and apart from girls in whose society I was both bashful and awkward. She was rather delicate, a very refined and intelligent woman of literary tastes and poetic instincts. Her make-up seemed just the opposite to my own rugged, untempered and uncultivated nature.

But Mary Jane found him attractive enough to accept when he proposed. They were married the following spring, May 22, 1856. Many well-meaning friends questioned Mary Jane's wisdom in choosing to marry one she had known such a short time and who seemed so different from her. But Mary Jane never regretted her decision and later wrote:

> Our marriage has proved that it was no mistake, and that contrary to the ideas of many, sudden attachments are often happy ones. I had a strong manly arm to lean on for comfort and support; and his wisdom and good natural intelligence gained him a position of trust and honor in the Church and in society.

Mary Jane and Myron lived in Peteetneet, afterwards known as Payson, seventy miles south of Salt Lake City, where Myron raised cattle and horses. In 1860, they settled permanently in Provo, where Myron purchased a gristmill and two farms. They became the parents of nine children, six of whom survived childhood: Joseph Marion, Bertrand, Mary Elizabeth (Bessie), Grace Lillian, Lewis, and Arthur.

Mary Jane continued to nurture her fondness for literature and poetry throughout her life. She wrote life sketches of the female descendants of the ruling houses of Europe for publication in the *Woman's Exponent* and she fulfilled a lifelong dream when she published a collection of her poetry, *Fugitive Poems,* in 1880.

Myron served as bishop of the Provo Third Ward and Mary Jane was called in 1868 as president of the ward Relief Society, a calling she held for twenty-two years.

The demands of husband, family, and church took their toll. Mary Jane could find only a little time to write and this was a constant frustration to her. She frequently fought bouts of discouragement, brought on by what seemed to her the never-ending drudgery of domestic chores and her inability to find enough time for her literary interests. In addition, her husband married a second wife and this created problems that became progressively harder for her to bear.

A small, thin sparrow of a woman, Mary Jane described herself as being "weak in constitution but strong in spirit, with more ambition than strength to carry out." Her lively personality was saddened to some degree by the deaths of three of her children, by the negative treatment she received at the hands of her step-mother and step-father, and by poor health.

When she died at age fifty-three, on January 12, 1903, she left an excellent autobiography, several diaries, and a collection of many letters written by her to other members of her family.

In her own words, Mary Jane's life was "a busy one: rearing my children and seeking to do a little good in my humble way. I have always held a good social position wherever I have resided: not a leader of fashion, but one of refinement, loving the society of the intelligent people. I have never been accustomed to luxury but have lived comfortably, except through the general persecution of the Church."

Ever anxious to leave some mark of her existence, Mary Jane wrote the following poem in the introduction to her book *Fugitive Poems*, expressing her sentiment toward her reader:

'Tis the child of my brain, and by labors brought forth
Should its pages contain either merit or worth,
Give the hearts of my friends either pleasure or gain,
I shall feel that my pen has not labored in vain.

'Tis a labor of love that my heart would bestow,
And the moments improve of my life as I go;
That when I am gone and my hands are at rest
My memory will live then in hearts I love best.

11

Sariah Louisa Chamberlain Redd

Undaunted Through Danger and Hardship

The family of Lemuel H. Redd, Sr. had spent every
available evening during the spring of 1865 picking wool until it was
clean and fluffy and then carding it into rolls. Now, they had
arranged for help to come in a few days to spin the huge rolls of bats
into woolen thread.

On the appointed day, a knock came at the door of the Redd
home in southern Utah. When they opened it, there stood sixteen-
year-old Sariah Louisa Chamberlain. In one hand she held a cloth
bag carrying her personal belongings, and in the other her spinning
wheel.

Louisa was a slight, black-eyed, quick-moving sixteen-year-old
who moved from task to task with speed and confidence, and the
family was delighted to have her help. She had a ready laugh. Eight-
year-old Jane Redd was captivated while watching Louisa spin: "I
was amused to watch her deftly twist those rolls into yarn as she
cleverly manipulated the wheel, running the treadles with her feet
and using both hands to twist and run the bobbins. I never tired
watching the spindle fill with the woolen thread."

When her spinning hours were over, Louisa helped with the
cooking, washed dishes, scrubbed floors and walls, and cared for
the children. As she worked alongside the Redd children, they

enjoyed her comradely manner. She chatted with them freely, making even the younger ones feel as if they were her equal in age. They soon learned how difficult her life had been during her first sixteen years.

Louisa's father, Solomon Chamberlain, had been one of the first converts to the Church and was among those settlers who had been expelled from Missouri by mob violence. He was among the original group of pioneers who entered the Salt Lake Valley in 1847. In spite of sickness, he had driven Brigham Young's carriage much of the way. He made a living as a cooper, turning out barrels, wooden tubs, and buckets that were eagerly sought throughout the countryside. He married Teresa Morse, a direct descendant of Samuel F. B. Morse, inventor of the telegraph, and Louisa was the only child from this union.

When Louisa was seven years old, her mother fell in love with another man and deserted the family, leaving Louisa to care for her aged father. She fed him, kept him clean, and cheered him when he was downcast. She was the epitome of the "poor little match girl."

Young Louisa proved to be a loving and capable caretaker for her father, literally saving his life on more than one occasion. One night, while they were living in Cedar City, eleven-year-old Louisa awoke to the smell of smoke and found their home in flames. Her father leaning on her for support, they made it safely out of the house. Louisa returned to carry out their most needed possessions; other more sentimental treasures were hurriedly crammed into a little black chest and were also spared from the flames.

Having lost their home, they moved from Cedar City and into a small adobe building in Santa Clara, Utah, where Solomon set up his workbench and tried to make a living. But his health was poor—he was crippled with rheumatism—and Louisa again shouldered most of the burden of caring for both of them. Had it not been for his resourceful daughter, Solomon's plight would have been considerably worse.

Just as they began to have more hope and courage, another disaster struck that destroyed what few comforts they had left. For eleven days it rained heavily, and every stream was threatening to overflow. Fearing to wait much longer, Louisa crossed a crude bridge across the Santa Clara river to the fort on the other side to get some yeast. She set a stake at the water's edge to measure its depth; when she returned, she was alarmed to see how quickly it was rising.

"We've got to move, and quick!" Louisa told her father as she rushed into their home and began gathering their most essential needs. These she piled on her father's workbench under a tree in the highest part of the yard. Again she grabbed her little black chest, which held her most valuable possessions, and lifted it into a crotch high in the tree.

As she returned to the house for her father, he refused to go. Solomon was in severe pain from his rheumatism and felt despondent, having lost much of his will to live. But under Louisa's gentle persuasion, he hobbled out, painfully climbing onto the workbench and into the tree where Louisa made him as comfortable as possible with quilts, coats, and pillows.

They spent the next thirty-six hours in the tree as the water swirled around them. They were chilled and cramped, but safe. The flood destroyed their home and many others around them, melting the adobe walls and carrying roofs away. Excited and bewildered people ran up and down the banks calling to the Chamberlains, saying that they would help if they could. But the water formed a virtual sea around the tree Louisa and her father were clinging to.

Finally, two nights and a day after they had fled to the tree from their home, the sun came out and help came in the form of a friendly Indian rowing by in his canoe. After several unsuccessful attempts, the Indian succeeded in lassoing the tree and mooring his canoe against its trunk while Louisa helped Solomon make a painful descent into it. The Indian gave them a loaf of bread, which looked like manna from heaven to their hungry eyes. Louisa later humorously recalled, "Yes, I've been driven out, burned out, flooded out, and I guess I've had my share of being bawled out."

Several offers were quickly made to provide shelter for the sick and elderly father, and they accepted the first, to the home of John D. Lee. Solomon lived only a few more days, but died full of appreciation for his daughter and others who had tried to make his last years as comfortable as possible.

Louisa was thirteen when her father died, and from that age, to use her words, she "just lived around wherever I could find work."

In 1865 she came to work at the Redd household, and a year later she became a plural wife of the head of the household, Lemuel H. Redd, Sr. "Pap," as Lemuel was affectionately called by his children, bought a home in Toquerville for Louisa to live in, but he eventually bought the large two-story home of John D. Lee on the headwaters of Ash Creek so all his family could live under one roof. Louisa and Keziah—Lemuel's first wife—worked together to keep the household running smoothly. Louisa eventually had fourteen children and Keziah thirteen, so there was plenty of sewing, cooking, and tending to do.

They later moved to New Harmony, southwest of Cedar City, Utah, and in 1874 that community entered the United Order. Lemuel became its vice-president and secretary. He also pulled teeth, was a practical veterinarian, and served as ward chorister.

A year and a half after Brigham Young's death, President John Taylor began urging Latter-day Saints to settle the useable farm and grazing land of southeastern Utah's San Juan region while it was still available. Latter-day Saint settlements could help establish friendly relations with the Indians and do missionary work among them.

So, in what proved an epic journey, the San Juan Mission in southeastern Utah was launched. Louisa's husband was one of four scouts who had been sent ahead of the other eighty families to blaze a trail from the Colorado River to Montezuma. The scouting trip should have taken eight days but ended only after twenty-four harrowing days of exploration involving near starvation and freezing temperatures.

The route they forged to Bluff, Utah, where Lemuel hoped to settle his family, took them through one of the most forbidding regions in western America. As one settler later wrote, "It's the roughest country you or anybody else ever seen; it's nothing in the world but rocks and holes, hill and hollows. The mountains are just one solid rock as smooth as an apple."

The settlers successfully accomplished the incredible feat of lowering scores of wagons through a treacherous ravine appropriately called Hole-in-the-Rock. Actually, it is not a "hole" at all, but a narrow steep cut in the west wall of Glen Canyon. First came a sheer drop of almost one hundred feet, then a little less steep decline of another three hundred feet. Steps had been carved into the sandstone for footing. With ropes tied to the wagons and held by twenty men and boys, each wagon was slowly guided down the "hole." Jagged rocks tore at the feet of the horses and cattle. Slowly, painfully, the entire company of 230 persons, their wagons, provisions, and livestock made their way down to the river below.

Finally, after nearly six months of constant road building and travel, they reached the lower San Juan. Shortly thereafter, "Pap" came to get Louisa and the rest of the family who had not made the first journey to Bluff. Because of its inaccessibility, Bluff protected the family from much of the tension and misery they and others had endured from anti-polygamy raids.

Eventually the family moved to Colonia Juarez, Mexico, where, from the money earned from the sale of their property in Utah, they built a spacious brick home. The family lived there in comfort, and Louisa made their home into a showplace with her gardening and homemaking skills. The floors were covered with carpets she wove, and doors were faced with rugs she had hooked.

From adjacent hills she dug ferns and fauna and transplanted them around her home, building rock gardens, terraces, and mounds for them, reproducing the beauty of the mountains in her own garden. She used potted plants and window boxes, filled with cuttings from a neighbor's choice plants, to build her scheme of beauty.

She taught her children to work as hard and swiftly as she did "or suffer the scathings of a haranguing tongue," one child would later recall. She was a famous scolder, and her tongue always kept pace with her hands and feet as she drove herself and her children through mountains of work each day.

Louisa Chamberlain Redd died of pneumonia March 7, 1907, in Mexico at the age of fifty-eight. Her children and grandchildren carried on her industrious traits, her delightful sense of humor, and her ambitious desire to achieve. Among her grandchildren is President Marion G. Romney, First Counselor in the First Presidency of the Church.

12

Sarah Endiaetta Young Vance
From Plantation Daughter to Arizona Midwife

Sarah Endiaetta Young came from a family of doctors. Her father, brother, and uncle all entered the medical profession and spent many hours traveling by buggy to visit patients in and around thinly populated Smyth County, Virginia, where Sarah was born November 24, 1861.

Sarah was the youngest of the sixteen children of Matilda Shepherd and Absolom McDonald Young. The family was well-to-do and enjoyed a happy homelife in a comfortable home on their 1600-acre plantation.

Sarah was generally unaware of the Civil War, which raged on during the early years of her childhood. She occasionally heard guns firing in the distance, and the family was frequently visited by soldiers seeking food, water, horses, and feed for their own livestock.

Most of the family's well-to-do neighbors worked their land with slaves, but Sarah's father "thought it was very wrong for one human being to own another" and refused to use slave labor.

The Young plantation was dotted with huge beautiful trees: chestnut, walnut, magnolia, maple, and a variety of fruit trees. When the sugar maple trees were tapped to make syrup, Sarah eagerly waited for the last batch, which was saved to make candy for the children. Endless stacks of buckwheat pancakes, dripping with the homemade syrup, were devoured by the large family around a sturdy oak table.

Many pleasant evenings were spent around the fire as the family roasted chestnuts. The dwarf chestnuts or "chinquapins" were much smaller and were fed to the hogs just before hog-killing day in the fall.

In the great trees were the perfect places for a young girl to play. Sarah took the moss which covered the trunk of a tree, rolled it into large balls, and put it up into the low forks of a tree. By arranging it over the wide-spreading branches, she built a floor for a playhouse. There, Sarah played for hours with her acorn dolls, dressing them in homemade clothes and acting out various nursery rhymes.

Sarah was still climbing trees and catching fireflies in jars when she first showed signs of wanting to be a doctor. She followed her father around in his "deep" study, intrigued by the large, heavy volumes of medical terms and diagrams. Her father's "drug room" contained shelf after shelf of medicines, some of which he compounded himself from herbs and other ingredients, but most of which were purchased. From this drug room, Sarah was allowed to borrow small bottles which she filled with water and pretended to administer to her ailing dolls.

Sarah's compassion for the sick resulted from her own personal battles against illness. She described at least two occasions in her youth when she became so sick she nearly died:

> I must have been about eight years old when I took the Spotted Mountain Fever, the kind that is carried by the bite of a woodtick. I remember well the day I was taken sick. That night we had green corn for supper. I dearly loved green corn, and still do today, but on that night I could eat none of it.

Sarah had just turned sixteen when she came down with typhoid fever. While tossing and turning in bed and "burning up with fever," Sarah had a vision which had personal meaning for the remainder of her life:

> I could see beautiful snow-covered mountains and other scenes of unimaginable beauty. Then I became aware that someone was standing at the foot of my bed. This person said, "Come! I want to show you something." I followed him into a big, spacious valley. It was like a huge amphitheatre with thousands of people sitting all around. On a

platform my father was speaking to them. I do not remember what he
said. I only know that he was preaching the Gospel. I was then shown
my future family. There were seven boys in the front row. Behind them
were other children whom I could not see distinctly enough so that I
could tell who they were. I knew though that they were going to be
mine. The vision vanished and I was back in my own room again.

Sarah clung to her dream of helping the sick even though female
doctors were still quite rare at the time. Her parents encouraged her
inquisitive mind and sought every opportunity to help her learn
more about medicine. They never dreamed, however, that the
achievement of her goal would begin first with a visit from two
Mormon missionaries.

Elder Dusenberry and his companion had come to Virginia from
Utah and arranged several cottage meetings to preach the news of
the "restoration of the gospel" by the now-martyred prophet,
Joseph Smith. They carried with them a copy of the Book of
Mormon, the new scripture which, they said, the Prophet had
translated from ancient gold plates.

Even before Sarah's family had been introduced to the
missionaries, they were favorably impressed with the new religion.
Sarah's father had become acquainted with a Mormon family in
another community while caring for a patient, and had, in fact,
named Sarah after a "cute little Mormon girl" four years before
hearing the missionaries preach. The Youngs were sympathetic to
the elders' message, acquired a testimony of the truthfulness of
Mormonism, and were baptized in 1865.

The Youngs' newfound happiness was temporarily dampened,
however, with the sudden death of Sarah's beloved father. Absolom,
called out on a particularly bitter-cold winter night to visit a patient,
had contracted pneumonia. During the last few days of his fight for
life, Absolom made his wife promise she would take the children
and join the Saints in Utah, thus avoiding the rejection they would
surely suffer if they stayed in Virginia.

After his death in 1865, Sarah's mother made plans to sell the
plantation and livestock for enough money to make the trip west.
Because the Youngs were Latter-day Saints, however, they were
unable to get a fair price for their property and ended up receiving
less than $600 for their animals, home, furniture, and the 1600-acre
plantation.

The Youngs joined many other emigrants in St. Louis, Missouri, and with them made the long journey to the Salt Lake Valley by train, the railroad having been finished in 1869. The welcome they received at the train station in Salt Lake City was less than encouraging. One can only guess what went through young Sarah's mind as she looked out the window of the train at the station platform, which was "covered with millions and millions of crickets." Sarah describes the whole town as being black with them. "Right there some of the Saints who had not been so well converted got back on the next train and returned to their home in the East."

One of Sarah's older brothers had already arrived in Utah several months earlier and had rented a home for his family in Fairview, ninety miles south of Salt Lake City. It was in this small farming community of about two hundred families that Sarah's family permanently settled.

The adjustments to this new way of life were difficult. They had lived prosperously in the South, growing fine field crops and orchards in rich, fertile soil. Another adjustment was required by the presence of Indians. Sarah never did get over her fear of them. She frequently heard stories of Indians "sneaking up" and killing settlers while they tended their cattle. Parents constantly warned their youngsters against wandering off by themselves into the woods or straying too far from a supervising adult. Difficult as it was, Sarah came to terms with the new way of life and adjusted successfully.

By the time Sarah was twelve years old in 1873, she did what many girls did to earn extra money; she hired out to work in the homes of other families. There was frequently a need for extra help, especially in homes where the children were too small to do much work or when a new baby arrived and the mother was temporarily unable to do her usual chores. Sarah did everything from washing clothes and ironing to fixing meals and general housecleaning. She recorded in her autobiography that "wages in those days were small and if I got $1.50 a week I was doing well." Sometimes her wages were not paid in cash at all but in produce or other goods. For example, when Sarah was about fifteen, she cared for a family of five or six children while their parents went to Salt Lake City. "I did all the work and took care of the milk and made butter. When they returned at the end of twelve days I had made enough butter to pay my wages."

By this time, Sarah was a young lady and became more interested in wearing attractive clothes and mingling with the young
men. In fact, at the age of fifteen she walked six and one-half miles
to buy her first store-sold hat. She must have felt that the trek was
worth it, because on the way home she met her first beau and he
offered to give her a ride. Sarah described the arrangements they
made on the way home for a future date:

> I had already made a date with this boy's brother to go horseback-
> riding on the next Sunday. Now when he was bringing me home this
> boy said that his brother was not able to go riding on the next Sunday
> and that he would like to take me in his stead. I agreed, but after we had
> gone on Sunday, this first brother came along to keep his date. You see,
> the other brother had storied me. I was so angry at him for that trick
> that nothing he could do would reconcile me to him.

Another would-be beau could have improved the impression he
made on Sarah if he had left his chewing tobacco at home:

> I sat behind him (on a horse, while horsebackriding) and he chewed
> tobacco. His breath made me so sick that I couldn't stand to be near
> him. I never went anywhere with him again. I did not even let him come
> into the house when we got home that afternoon.

Sarah had a soft heart, which kept her in constant fear of hurting
a boy's feelings by turning him down for a date. She even became
engaged to a young man she didn't particularly like after thinking
about how disappointed he would be if she said "no."

Luckily, a week after her engagement, John Vance spotted Sarah
at Sunday School and immediately made plans to win her heart.
John had lived in Fairview as a young boy but had since moved to
St. George. He was now in Fairview with a load of dried fruit which
he hoped to exchange for other produce.

John secretly found out where Sarah was going to be that afternoon and made arrangements to be introduced. Sarah recorded in
her autobiography what happened after that:

> I spent that afternoon with John. Now this other boy (the one to
> whom I was engaged), had failed to make a date with me to go to church
> that night, taking it for granted that I would go with him. I liked John so
> much better than the other boy that I forgot all about him and made a
> date to go with John. Then the other boy came along and insisted that I
> walk home with him whether I wanted to or not. I knew what I wanted

though and even the pleadings of the other boy could not make me change my mind. [Later], when the other boy came and wanted to know what I meant by my attitude I simply told him that I did not love him and that was that.

John returned to St. George, but although they were separated by a hundred miles, he and Sarah continued their courtship by occasional visits and love letters.

Sarah Endiaetta Young and John Thomas Vance were married November 21, 1877, in the St. George Temple, three days before Sarah's sixteenth birthday. She and John moved in with his parents in St. George, but it turned out to be only a brief stay. Sarah was so young that leaving her mother and brothers and sisters was very difficult. "I was still only a sixteen-year-old child," she wrote. "I was now so homesick that nothing would do but that we return to my mother's home in Fairview." John consented and they moved to Fairview.

In 1879, however, shortly after the birth of their first child, a son, Sarah's husband had the urge to move to Arizona. He and others caught the "Arizona Fever," and the little family joined a group of Saints to settle first at Hayden's Ferry (Tempe) and then on the outskirts of the Mormon community of Mesa.

Sarah's married life was full of hardship, struggles, numerous moves, and just plain hard work. She and her husband worked together, from the ground up, to build a good life. They cleared the land for crops, dammed the canals to irrigate the fields, put up fences to keep livestock in, and built their first home, a one-room adobe house with dirt floor and roof. They felt lucky as years went by to add doors and windows, to shingle the roof, and to build a board floor. It was several years before John came home with their first piece of purchased furniture—a rocking chair.

Sarah made butter and cheese, milked cows, drove wagons, fed and watered the livestock, and raised chickens, turkeys, geese, and ducks to sell. This was in addition to ironing, cooking, cleaning, and caring for their ever-increasing family.

Danger was a fact of life. Terrifying desert wind and rainstorms blew the roofs off many homes and caused severe flooding. Irrigation canals occasionally claimed the life of a small toddler. For a woman alone at home, there were many frightening experiences. Sarah records:

One day as I sat in our one-room house rocking my baby, an immense six-foot rattlesnake came in through one door of the house, crawled all the way across the floor and out the opposite door. I sat perfectly still and it never diverged from its path. Scorpions and centipedes were an everyday occurrence and there were many snakes.

After fourteen years in Arizona, John and Sarah became discouraged with the hard life in this arid region and moved first to Sanford, Colorado, a barren, cold place with bedbugs, then to the Uinta Basin, which was so cold that Sarah remembers scraping frost from their bedposts. They finally decided that Arizona was not so bad after all and returned to their farm, which they had rented out during their absence.

During their trip from the Uinta Basin back to Arizona, John and Sarah stopped for a while in Salt Lake City to attend quarterly conference. They also went through the Salt Lake Temple for the first time. Sarah described how this stopover forever changed her life:

> While we were here (in Salt Lake City) I decided to stay and fulfill that dearest of my childhood ambitions when I desired above all else to be a doctor like my father when I grew up. I enrolled in a class for the study of obstetrics under Dr. Ellis R. Shipp.

With the full support of her husband, Sarah rented a room in Salt Lake City across the hall from Dr. Shipp while John returned to Arizona. Her determination to complete the course is evidenced by the fact that she was willing to keep her three youngest sons with her, contending with the inconveniences that resulted from such an arrangement, while the other children went on to Arizona with John. She later wrote of the challenge the children presented:

> You can just imagine what a time I had with those three lively little country boys in the city. I would lock them into the room while I attended my classes. No sooner was I gone than out through the window would go Leslie and Bert, leaving the baby alone. . . . Of course, they got themselves into all kinds of little troubles too. One day they came home chewing gum which they had picked up on the street. I told them stories of how they would get sore throats and mouths and they quit only to take up something else. Once a policeman came up to tell me that I would have to keep those boys off the street. That was more than I could manage. They never did anything bad; they were just mischievous little boys.

Sarah graduated six months later with a diploma declaring her fully competent to be a midwife. Elder Abraham H. Cannon, an Apostle of the Church, gave her a gracious and reassuring blessing, promising that she would have a "Guardian Angel" to watch over her and guide her in her work so that she would always do only what was right and what was best for the welfare of her patients.

Sarah returned to her family in Arizona and began her medical practice. As her reputation as an excellent midwife spread throughout the region, many called on her for help in cases other than the delivering of a child. She restored the health of a young girl stricken with typhoid fever whom the doctor had given up to die. She nursed her own children through diphtheria as well as numerous cases of infection and injury. She applied artificial respiration to two of her toddlers who nearly drowned, thus saving their lives.

Sarah was particularly proud of a special "solution" which she used successfully for a host of ailments—everything from a splintered leg to a severed finger to head injuries her son suffered after falling off a horse. Her special recipe was: "To one pint each of water and vinegar, add two ounces of spirits of camphor and about a teaspoonful of turpentine. Just saturate a towel or bandage and keep it on the affected parts."

Sarah loved her work as a midwife and spent the next forty-five years serving people in Arizona with her excellent medical skills. Her record was remarkable: she delivered approximately fifteen hundred babies and never lost one child or mother. Frequently she was called out three times in twenty-four hours, and she was proud of the fact that she found it necessary to call for the services of a physician only six times in all those years.

When asked to tell the secret of her success, she replied:

> I cannot explain it. I only know that whenever I came up against a difficult problem something always seemed to inspire me and somehow I would know what was the right thing to do. It may have been instinct or just good common sense. Something guided me the right way.

Sarah was respected and sought-after for her advice on a variety of subjects. Local church leaders even asked for her opinion on the design of a new chapel to be built in Mesa. Because of her valued contribution, they also asked her to speak at the ground-breaking ceremonies and help lay the cornerstone.

Sarah and John Vance eventually tired of the hard ranch life and in 1906 moved into the town of Mesa itself. They soon noticed that teenagers were taking the train into Phoenix to find the entertainment that Mesa did not offer. John saw the need to provide something for the young people to do and from this idea the Vance Auditorium developed. The hall, which is now known as the Mezona, held road and moving picture shows, vaudeville acts, dances, and skating parties.

Sarah and John became the parents of thirteen children, including two sets of twins. They served faithfully in the Church, John being called on a mission to the southern states and later serving for many years as a Sunday School superintendent. Sarah was Relief Society president and a member of the stake Relief Society board.

Sarah's beloved companion, John, died in 1928. Sarah spent her remaining years serving the Church, visiting and taking trips with her children and grandchildren, doing handwork, and occasionally delivering babies. Many times in her later life, women came to Sarah and profoundly thanked her for helping them when their babies were born. Many felt she had saved their lives or the lives of their children.

The dream of the small girl who lived on a plantation in Virginia was richly fulfilled. Like her father, brothers, and uncle, she had spent a life of service in the medical profession, though she had had to cross most of a continent and endure much hardship to do it. Surely the thanks of the women whose lives and children she had helped spare brought much personal satisfaction.

Sarah Endiaetta Young Vance died November 19, 1940, in Mesa, Arizona, at the age of seventy-nine.

13

Catherine Heggie Griffiths
A Century in Cache Valley

The life of Catherine Walker Stewert Heggie Griffiths spanned a remarkable one hundred one years. She was privileged to observe and participate in a century-long transformation of Cache Valley, Utah-Idaho. When she was born, it was a pioneer settlement of about two thousand settlers and a few Indians; by the time she died it was a thriving agricultural and commercial valley of nearly thirty communities, with a population of more than fifty thousand, and had become the home of Utah State University.

The year Catherine was born, 1867, Brigham Young was President of the Church, the Relief Society was organized under Eliza R. Snow, and United States President Andrew Johnson had just finalized the purchase of Alaska. Catherine saw the Church grow in membership from fewer than a hundred thousand to more than three million, saw the Logan Temple built and dedicated, and saw the horse-and-buggy days fade into the era of commercial air travel and Apollo moon shots.

Catherine's parents, Andrew Walker Heggie and Annie Thompson Stewert, were among a dozen families called by Elder Ezra T. Benson, an Apostle, in 1864 to help settle a new community in the northwest end of Cache Valley. They went under the leadership of Israel J. Clark, who directed them in building the dugouts and the few rough log cabins in which they spent their first winter. The new settlement was named "Clarkston"; the Heggies' first child, Annie, was the first child born in the new little community. Catherine was born two years later on March 4, 1867, after the family had moved into the new Clarkston Fort, which had been built to protect the settlers from the troublesome Shoshoni Indians. The fort was two blocks long with a street six rods wide through the center and a stream of water running down each side, the houses fronting upon the street, and cattle corrals and sheds outside.

As Indian problems subsided, Catherine's father built a one-room log home for his family a short distance from the fort. Catherine and her sister Annie made a lengthy hike each day to take their father his dinner, resting along the way on the banks of a creek.

Catherine's childhood home had a rough lumber floor and a roof made of layers of willows, straw, and dirt. Beds were made of strips of rawhide stretched across a frame which held a straw tick and homemade linsey sheets. The morning after a bad rainstorm, Catherine and her brothers and sisters would wake up to find several pans on their beds, catching the water as it dripped through the roof.

Cache Valley winters were often severe; the settlers had to cope with winds, deep snow, and temperatures well below zero. Wind whistling through cracks in the cabin walls was a common sound. Bread dough set out the night before to rise was often found frozen the next morning.

Catherine's upbringing was one of strict discipline, her Scottish parents insisting on respect and honor within the home and believing in obedience to the laws of the gospel. The family prayed together frequently and the children were taken by the hand to Sunday meetings each week.

The Heggie children were not allowed to "roam around" with other children their own age. Once when Catherine was picking chokecherries and wandered further away from home than she was allowed to, her mother made her beg on her knees for forgiveness.

Her mother's conservative temper led her to be particularly wary of new fads and fashions, and she was always conscious of what was considered proper and improper behavior. Two Clarkston girls once strolled into church on Sunday morning wearing the first tailored coats in town, which had been made and purchased in Corinne.

Catherine's mother thought they looked rather "mannish" and called them "brazen hussies," but it wasn't long before many women were wearing such attire. Several winters later, Catherine's parents, on their way home from having dinner at a friend's house, were passed by a noisy group of teenagers sleigh riding and singing at the top of their voices. Catherine's mother remarked to those near her, "There goes a lot of hoodlums," without knowing that Catherine was among them.

Along with the strict upbringing she endured, Catherine was given a great deal of love and affection. She adored her parents. She later wrote: "What pleasant memories come to me of my mother as I think back of her planning to make our life pleasant. I thought there was no one so smart or as beautiful. And [I think] of father as he would sit in the evening with the smallest one on his knee and sing the songs each of us would select for him."

Such feelings of love and security were especially important because pioneer life was commonly full of terrifying experiences, danger, and death. Many babies died before they were a year old; of those who survived infancy, about one-fourth died before they reached sixteen. Catherine was one of five children; William, the youngest in the family, died at the age of two. Of her own eight children, one boy died of pneumonia twelve days after his birth and a girl died of diphtheria at age six. Death and danger were ever-present realities through disease, accidents, and improper protection from the elements.

The Indians were almost a daily problem for some settlers, and most children were terrified of them. Although the Indians usually only wanted food or supplies, there were occasional incidents of attempted kidnappings and assaults. Catherine always scurried to hide behind her mother's skirt when they came "lurking around." Catherine describes how a small group of Indians became particularly attached to her little brother, Willie: "Often in fruit time they would gather a pan of chokecherries or serviceberries to sell to mother [and] they were pleased when our baby brother Willie would go to them. They would pick a large cluster of cherries and give them to him. The next summer they came again with fruit and asked for the little papoose. When told he had died that winter they were very sad, and shook their heads from side to side."

As the railroad came through Cache Valley in the 1870s, transients and indigent workers frequently wandered to nearby homes seeking food; their presence became a source of concern for the young people and their parents. Once Catherine remained at home while the rest of the family attended their Sunday Church meetings: "I stayed in the house for some time until I got scared of the silence, then I went for a walk around the lot. I was frightened there too and began to wonder if I would be killed by some tramp or some other harmful person, and was sure glad when the family got home from meeting. I never wanted to stay home alone after that experience."

The elements could also pose a great danger to the settlers. Seven-year-old Catherine became terrified during a particularly bad windstorm after it had blown the roof off the nearby general store: "I was only a small girl, but [I] can remember how frightened I was. I lay awake most of the night thinking our house would be blown to bits. Mother found out how scared I was and lay her hand on my head to reassure me and soon I went to sleep."

Pioneer life was by its very nature full of hard work. Even the young children were expected to help with the chores. The Heggies had a small flock of sheep, and Catherine and her sisters helped in every aspect of cloth making from tending the sheep in the hills to the final hand-sewing of their clothes. Their reward for "picking" the wool until it was clean and fluffy was an egg for each child, which they took to the co-op store and traded for hard-tack candy made into shapes of fishes, elephants, dogs, and soldiers.

Catherine was baptized on August 8, 1875, "for the remission of sins and into the United Order" by Martin Harris, Jr., son of one of the three witnesses to the Book of Mormon. She was confirmed the same day by Andrew McCombs.

As the years went by and everyone became more prosperous, Catherine was able to participate in more elaborate social experiences with her friends. She was especially fond of dancing and many opportunities to learn to dance were provided by the community for even the youngest citizens. "Brother James Myler used to manage the children's dances when I was small," Catherine wrote. "He was a regular good fellow with the children and would see that all had a chance to dance. He came to me one dance, when I was standing alone, too bashful to dance. He took me across the floor, and left me to ask a partner for the dance. I asked the first one on the bench, he refused to dance. So I asked the next, and he refused. I kept on until I asked them all. Will was at the end and he danced with me. He later became my husband."

Catherine was proud of her ability to dance the Highland Fling, frequently performing this dance between acts of a drama being held to raise money for various organizations. She describes her dancing costume: "The dress I wore . . . was a short full skirt, low neck, short sleeved white dress with rosette soft pumps with red ribbon laced around my legs to the knee. My hair was in ringlets [with] a wreath of artificial roses. I later made a Scottish highland kilt for dancing the Highland Fling."

Catherine also enjoyed playing ball. "I used to be able to knock the ball as far as any one, and I was a good catcher too." Her mother, however, disapproved of her participation in the ball games, saying she wore out her shoes too quickly. She soon insisted that Catherine play barefoot, thinking she would stop, but Catherine would make moccasins from old pieces of cloth. Her mother finally let Catherine wear her shoes again while playing.

Catherine started school at the early age of four and attended for ten years, making her more fortunate than many others at the time. But the process of learning seems to have been a slow one. She later wrote that she had gone to school for six years before she knew her ABCs, and she was not allowed to begin reading until she had the alphabet learned. She studied reading, writing, and spelling until she was eleven and then was taught arithmetic, geography, and grammar.

When she was thirteen, Catherine took a special handwriting course from a Mrs. Alfred White. She wrote of her frustration in not being able to perform as well as she wanted to: "[The teacher] had each pupil write a specimen of his penmanship and hand it in with his name signed to it. I wrote the very best I could [and] all the other pupils just scribbled. They all got excellent marks. I got none."

Several highlights of Catherine's school experience were the plays she participated in. Her stage debut was made in "The Imps of the Trunk Room" and she later had parts in "The Drunkard's Wife," "The Tom Boy," and "The Rose of Etric Vale." These experiences not only provided pleasant social experiences ("we usually had a lot of fun at our practices'') but also served to build Catherine's self-confidence in speaking and reciting prose and poetry. She memorized scores of poems and throughout her life gave recitations at social gatherings and at various church meetings. When Catherine was eighty-eight years old, a family member wrote that she could still recite twenty poems by heart.

In 1880, a new co-op store was built in Clarkston for which Catherine's father was chosen as the clerk. Thirteen-year-old Catherine and her sister frequently assisted him at the store, and it was here that William Griffiths began to court her. Acting on a bet he had with his stepbrother, Will asked Catherine to go to a dance with him. She accepted. He not only won the bet, but continued to court her by escorting her to sleigh-riding parties and to a circus in Logan, and by taking her home from her night penmanship class. They eventually married on January 6, 1886, in the Logan Temple.

Catherine and Will became the parents of eight children, six of whom lived to maturity. They moved to Trenton, twelve miles east of Clarkston, shortly after they were married. They lived there ten years before returning to Clarkston. Will farmed while Catherine supplemented the family income by boarding schoolteachers.

Catherine served as secretary in the Clarkston Relief Society for twenty years and was frequently involved with homemaking demonstrations on cooking and sewing. She also received a special calling when she was set apart to sew burial clothes for the dead.

Catherine had a special interest in history, enjoying her membership in the Daughters of the Utah Pioneers, of which she served both as captain and as historian of the Martin Harris Camp. She was a dedicated genealogist who helped many with their personal and family histories.

The citizens of Clarkston frequently honored Catherine at their community celebrations as one of its earliest native-born pioneers. She rode in numerous parades, both in Clarkston and in Logan, and took part in various programs put on by the school, church, and community. She remained independent and busy throughout her later years and enjoyed crocheting, sewing, and making quilts.

Of all the technological advancements Catherine saw in her lifetime, the one she seemed to appreciate the most was the automobile. She and Will bought their first car in 1916 and enjoyed various excursions to Yellowstone Park, the Snake River, the national parks in southern Utah, and the Grand Canyon.

Her husband died in 1934, leaving Catherine a widow for the last thirty-four years of her life. She died April 14, 1968, and is buried in Clarkston, Utah, just a short distance from where she was born more than a century earlier.

Part Four

Second-Generation Achievers

14

Lula Greene Richards

Poet, Journalist, Editor

One afternoon twenty-two-year-old Louisa Lula Greene was called into the family home in Smithfield, Utah. Her mother handed her a letter which had just arrived from Salt Lake City. It was addressed to Lula (the name by which she was most commonly known) from Edward L. Sloan, the esteemed editor of the *Salt Lake Herald*. Lula had published various poems in the *Herald* and expected this to be, perhaps, a request for more material. Instead, the letter would change Lula's life and the lives of many women throughout the Church. Sloan wrote that many prominent Mormon women felt the time was right to establish a newspaper, exclusively by and for women, to give them a periodical to express their views and sentiments. Lula was their candidate for the editorship.

Feeling complimented but unqualified, Lula declined the offer. Sloan quickly wrote back, saying it was the quality of her writing that had inspired the idea of the newspaper and that if she declined the editorship, the entire project would probably be abandoned.

After much consideration, Lula wrote that if Eliza R. Snow approved the project, and if her great-uncle, President Brigham Young, would call her to the editorship as a mission, she would accept. With the wholehearted endorsement of both, the *Woman's*

Exponent was born, and so was the professional career of Utah's first woman journalist.

Louisa Lula Greene was born Easter Sunday, April 8, 1849, the eighth of thirteen children born to Evan M. and Susan Kent Greene. Her parents were cousins; their mothers were both sisters to Brigham Young. Both parents were natives of New York and had joined the Church soon after its organization in 1830. Lula's father was a well-known educator who taught English grammar classes in Kirtland, Ohio, the Prophet Joseph Smith being one of his students.

Following the main body of Saints, the Greenes lived in Nauvoo for six years and then joined in the exodus westward, moving first to Kanesville, Iowa, on the banks of the Missouri River. Kanesville, named after Thomas L. Kane, a non-Mormon friend of the Saints, served as one of the major outfitting posts for western travellers. It was here, during a long siege of cholera among the Saints, that Lula was born. Although the new baby girl was healthy, the chances of her surviving were slim. Two other Greene children had already died as infants and more were to follow. But against all odds, Lula lived ninety-five years.

Lula was only four years old in 1852 when her family left Kanesville and made the long trek to the Salt Lake Valley. Lula never forgot two incidents that occurred along the way—events typical of the dangers thousands of young pioneers faced to resettle in the West.

At the beginning of the journey, little Lula fell from a raft ferrying their wagon across the Missouri River. Her dress caught on some nails protruding from the side of the boat, holding Lula just under the surface of the water, but keeping her from being swept away. Luckily, Brother Edwards, a Welsh neighbor, seeing the apparently lifeless form in the river, reached down and rescued her. Lula saw the hand of the Lord in her rescue, saying, ''I knew I was being taken care of.''

Some weeks later, Lula and her sister Nancy rode alone in the family wagon as their weary oxen pulled it up a steep embankment rising from a river they had just crossed. Just before reaching the top of the bluff, one of the oxen stumbled; the wagon detached and began slipping backwards. The two girls clung to each other, fearing for their lives. Near the bottom, however, the wagon swerved to one side and hit a stump, bringing the wagon to a halt, its contents shaken but intact, and the girls safe.

Upon arriving in Utah, the Greenes settled in Provo, forty-five miles south of Salt Lake City, where Lula's father taught school, served as mayor, and represented Utah County in the territorial legislature.

Lula manifested her spiritual nature as well as her strong will early in life. At the age of six, when witnessing the baptism of her elder sister, Lula cried to be baptized, too. After listening to her sobbing for some time, her parents finally gave in, allowing her to be baptized that same day. Lula was rebaptized, however, shortly after her eighth birthday.

The Greene family would move at least six times in the next dozen years. Lula seemed to weather the moves well, and wrote sentimental poems about the places they had lived. After leaving Provo the Greenes settled temporarily in Grantsville, where Lula's father served two terms in the legislature, representing Tooele County. They then moved to Bennington, in Bear Lake Valley, where Evan had been called by the Church to preside over the local branch. The family endured many hardships in this settlement, including the death of Lula's ten-year-old brother, Admanzah, and the death in childbirth of her older sister, Rhoda. As soon as her father was released from this calling, the family bought a farm in Smithfield, in Cache Valley, which was to be Lula's last childhood home.

Lula's education up to this point had come from her father at home. She was as much a student of his teaching techniques as of the subject matter he discussed and apparently inherited, or mastered, his natural ability with students. Though Lula enjoyed dancing, sleighing, and theatricals, she took greatest delight in teaching her younger brothers and sisters. Lula was eighteen when she and her sister Melissa opened a small school attended by the children of the neighborhood. Some school days went well; others tried her patience:

> June 11, 1867: "What trying things children are! especially boys; full of fun and mischief, and so ungenerous, ungrateful and tantalizing. . . . I haven't had a minute's rest all . . . afternoon. I don't see why they will be so mean! Oh hush, for shame Lula! They are children, have not the

wisdom, reason, forethought, nay, nor pride they will have when they are older. Must I not bear with their failings even as I ask my Heavenly Father to bear with mine? I want to but it is hard, very hard to be always patient and forebearing.

Lula fretted about her lack of formal education, which she felt she needed in order to properly handle the children. "I want to be a very good school teacher," she wrote, "and do not know how. I feel that I am not competent as yet to do justice in this respect and so am not satisfied with what I do."

Lula's dream of formal schooling was realized in January 1869, when her father took her to Salt Lake City to attend the Rogers and Tripp School. She enjoyed the school, respected her instructors, and was pleased with her progress.

Lula had written various stories and poems for children by this time, but now she became more earnest about becoming a journalist. As she sought to have some of her literary works published, her first efforts met with quick success. The *Salt Lake Herald* and the *Deseret News* bought and published several of her poems, and her name began appearing regularly in their weeklies.

Lula returned to Smithfield during the summer months, immersing herself in the activities of the community. Still only twenty, she was called to be secretary of the ward Relief Society and also taught a Sunday School class. Her involvement with the Sunday School brought Lula a perfect outlet for her writing talent—she founded and edited the *Smithfield Sunday School Gazette*. Sunday School manuscript newspapers were common in Latter-day Saint communities in the 1860s and 1870s. They were handwritten, two-column papers, usually on four to eight sheets of legal-size writing paper, and contained stories, poetry, and short sermonettes. They went under such names as the *Young Ladies Enterprize* (Honeyville, Utah), the *Young Ladies Companion* (Bountiful, Utah), and *The Knowledge Seeker* (Hyrum, Utah). Each paper also carried a motto such as "We Seek the Truth," "Knowledge Is Power," and "Remember Thy Creator In The Days of Thy Youth." The theme of Lula's first newspaper was "Attend Sunday School and Preserve Order."

These newspapers were often a forum for the views and concerns of the local citizens. For example, in September of 1888, an irate citizen in Hyrum, Utah, wrote:

What is more aggravating than for a person to fix up a garden then to have bad boys destroy it when he is asleep. Or to plant a nice melon patch, and before they get ripe, or even after they get ripe, then have them stolen and the vines destroyed.

I have had boys come to my garden a few nights ago and ravage my melon patch. When I was not able to get out of bed or stand on my feet and I have not been able for a week and they knew it. Such boys are not only thieves, but cowards of the worst order.

It is a pity that the law does not overtake them and learn them that trespassing on other people's ground is contrary to justice.

Most of the contributors to the *Gazette* and other manuscript newspapers were teenagers, although the bishop and other ward leaders were often called upon to contribute words of advice. The handwritten copy was available every Sunday or every other Sunday at the close of the service and was passed in turn among those who had paid the subscription price. The usual terms were: "Attend Sabbath School and pay attention."

While Lula was editor of the *Smithfield Gazette,* her father was the city recorder and the girls of the Retrenchment Association (the Mutual of those days) often met after school in his office to prepare their papers for the next Sunday. With a good sense of timing, Lula often came out with a special issue to celebrate the wedding anniversary of the oldest couple in the ward, or with a poem of praise to a young man who had just accepted a call to go on a mission. Sometimes the editorship was rotated among the girls so all could share its responsibilities and joys.

At twenty, Lula was an imposing, self-confident, and popular young woman. She had thick brown hair which hung in long curls down her back, was a slender five feet four inches, and usually wore a long-sleeved blouse with a high collar pinned with a broach. Her skirts were down to the ankles; her shoes were high-topped button or laced.

Lula, who enjoyed a close relationship with her brothers and sisters, spent many hours of her youth working with them at home. A granddaughter, Helen Richards Gardner, wrote of an incident Lula often enjoyed retelling:

Lula's sister, Melissa, and she were at home all day preparing the meals and doing the housework while the parents spent the day at the temple. There was a root cellar under the kitchen floor with a trap door right in the middle of the floor. Lula was starching the clothes in a large pan of starch water and Melissa was preparing dinner. Melissa lifted the trap door to get out potatoes from the pit. Lula, not realizing the door was open, stepped back, falling into the pit. As she fell she grabbed for the starch pan and it went over her head drenching her in starch water. Stunned she came up wet and gasping and sputtering through the starch water. "You old sot!" she sputtered. She was not hurt, but bruised, and soon the sight brought the two girls down in roars of laughter. What a mess the starchy potato pit was and what a sight was Lula with her brown curls drenched with starch. As one might expect, her curls soon became stiff as a board.

In 1870 Lula was released from her various callings in Smithfield to return to Salt Lake City for further training at the University of Deseret. Now twenty-one, Lula began to consider more seriously the direction her life should take. She was devoted to her family, but she was experiencing inner yearnings that set her apart from them. A poem she wrote at this time reflects her personal feelings:

> Did I stay too long in the school room
> After lessons were through
> Leaving my mother and sisters
> With all my work to do?
> And has it vexed you, mother
> My mother, so patient and true?
>
> Forgive me, my mother and sisters,
> Smile kindly and gently speak;
> I'll try to do better tomorrow
> And all the rest of the week.
> If my wayward mind and feelings
> Do not play me another freak.
>
> For I have been writing something
> Which will likely be read
> By our children's children
> After we all are dead;
> And must I think I should have been
> Washing dishes instead?

Lula enjoyed corresponding with Eliza R. Snow, whom she affectionately knew as "Aunt Eliza," and found her very supportive of Lula's desire to pursue a literary career. Even after Lula accepted the offer to edit the *Woman's Exponent,* one concern continued to nag at her. She was twenty-two years old—shouldn't she be getting married? Lula sought the advice of Aunt Eliza, who wrote back:

> To be sure, while unmarried, one cannot be fulfilling the requisition of maternity, but let me ask "Is it not as important that those already born be cultivated and prepared for use in the Kingdom of God as that others should be born?" If left to me to decide, I should say that of the two, the cultivation of the [mind] is the most consequence. How many mothers give birth to children who themselves are altogether unqualified to perform the duties of mothers? And yet, for Zion's sake, those children must be cultivated.

Encouraged with this advice and determined to do her best, Lula moved to Salt Lake City, issued a prospectus, and began to sell subscriptions to the *Exponent*. The first issue came out on June 1, 1872, when Lula was only twenty-three. The fact that it first appeared on Brigham Young's birthday must have pleased the pioneer leader.

For the first year and a half, the *Exponent* was put together in a small room in the home of Lorenzo Dow Young, Lula's great-uncle, with whom she boarded. Her office equipment consisted of a table with writing materials, a few books, some magazines, and several chairs. She was the editorial staff. In spite of such modest beginnings, history was being made—the *Exponent* was the first continuous newspaper published for and by women west of the Mississippi. The paper was published for forty-two years and then was replaced by the *Relief Society Magazine*.

In time, Lula's staff would expand to include an associate editor, a secretary, a business manager, a consulting committee, and an ever-increasing number of contributors. The *Exponent*'s bimonthly issues were read by several thousand women throughout the United States and Great Britain, and the ideas it discussed sparked lively exchanges with other women's journals.

During her five years as editor, Lula devoted editorials to such issues as her support of the women's suffrage movement, the health and education of children, home industry, and a generous amount of advice for parents, young women, and newlyweds on a variety of subjects.

On June 16, 1873, at the age of twenty-four, Lula married Levi W. Richards, a man described as being "of sterling integrity, of similar tastes, and of good family." Lula's granddaughter writes of how their engagement came about:

There were a group of boys and girls who went to the Mutual dances and walked home together. Of the group there were two or three who seemed attracted to Lula. They were forward and sometimes wanted to kiss her, but she wouldn't let them. One night after the dance, a bashful young man asked to see her home. He did, and proposed to her. She was surprised because she hadn't even thought of him as a suitor. He was not forward at all. She replied: "I will have to have a few days to pray about it." She went into the house and did pray. After a time she concluded that maybe she did love him. She hadn't thought much about him because he was so quiet, but why shouldn't she love him? She had never heard anything bad about him. So she decided she did love him and agreed to marry.

As children began to arrive at the Richards household, and as Lula began to experience health problems, she asked to be released as editor. On August 1, 1877, Lula published her final editorial. Her words did not signal an end to her writing career, only a change in direction:

> In announcing my exit from the editorial department of the *Woman's Exponent* I do not feel that I am bidding its patrons and readers "a long and sad farewell" but hope, as a contributor, to still communicate with them occasionally. . . .
>
> My general health is good, but my head and eyes need recruiting, and I have decided to humor them. I have also decided that during the years of my life which may be properly devoted to the rearing of a family I will give my special attention to that most important branch of "Home Industry." Not that my interest in the public weal is diminishing, or that I think the best season of a woman's life should be completely absorbed in her domestic duties. But every reflecting mother, and every true philanthropist can see the happy medium between being selfishly home bound, and foolishly public spirited.

Lula continued to write as she reared her family. Throughout her life she carried a notebook in her purse for writing when some thought entered her mind. Relatives recall that often an idea would come to her in the middle of the evening meal and Lula would get up from the table to write for several hours, oblivious of the work that needed to be done to wash the dishes, clean the house, or get children ready for bed. She often retreated to a small home on the back of their lot that had been previously occupied by her mother-in-law. This home became Lula's writing studio, where she could concentrate more deeply on her reading and writing.

Lula published poems and articles in the *Exponent*, the *Relief Society Magazine*, the *Children's Friend*, the *Improvement Era*, and the *Young Woman's Journal*, and conducted a department of the *Juvenile Instructor* under the heading "Our Little Folks." In 1904, when she was fifty-five, Lula published a book of verse entitled *Branches That Run Over the Wall*. The following year, in honor of the hundredth anniversary of the birth of the Prophet Joseph Smith, the Deseret Sunday School Union offered three prizes for the three best poems on the Prophet. Lula won all three prizes!

In addition to her literary activities, Lula bore seven children, of whom three daughters, Mary, Mabel, and Sarah, died in infancy. Four sons grew to manhood: Levi ("Lee") Greene became one of the West's most creative painters; Willard participated in the colonization and development of southern Alberta, Canada; Evan was a dentist; and Heber became a professor of English at the University of Utah.

While raising her family and continuing her writing, Lula also served as president of the Young Ladies' Mutual Improvement Association of the Twentieth Ward in Salt Lake City; as an officer of the Relief Society in that ward; as a member of the general board of the Primary Association of the Church; and as a member of the general board of the Deseret Sunday School Union. She was an officiator in the Salt Lake Temple from the time of its dedication in 1893 until 1934. To organize and inspire the women's auxiliaries, Lula represented the Church at meetings of women, young and old, from Canada to Mexico.

Few Latter-day Saints have excelled Lula Greene Richards in influence and versatility. She died in Salt Lake City in 1944 at the age of ninety-five.

15

Ellis Reynolds Shipp

Beehive House Schoolgirl Who Became a Pioneer Doctor

William Hawley picked up his heavy black medical bag and hoisted it into the back of his horse-drawn buggy. Then he turned and picked up his eager granddaughter, placing her gently on the front seat next to where he would be sitting. After climbing aboard, and with a quick shake of the reins, Grandpa Hawley began driving little Ellis Reynolds on their journey down the dusty farm road to visit a nearby settlement where medical assistance was needed.

"Brother Hawley" was well known throughout the Salt Lake Valley in the late nineteenth century for his skill in setting broken bones. As a young man, Hawley had attended medical school for a few months in Iowa, where he became proficient at this particular skill. He was often summoned to set broken bones, and dark-haired Ellis was a frequent and fascinated companion on such excursions.

Years later, as Ellis Reynolds Shipp, M.D., this granddaughter gained a reputation of her own as an expert setter of bones. She was quick to admit, with a twinkle in her eye, "I learned more from Grandfather about setting bones than I did in medical college."

Ellis Reynolds was born January 20, 1847, the same year the first Mormon pioneer company crossed the Great Plains to the Salt Lake Valley. She was the eldest child of William Fletcher Reynolds and Anna Hawley, who lived in Davis County, Iowa.

Soon after Ellis's birth, her parents heard and accepted the teachings of The Church of Jesus Christ of Latter-day Saints; they migrated to Utah in 1852, with five-year-old Ellis riding in the back of their covered wagon. One never-to-be-forgotten event of the crossing occurred on August 15, as the company camped at Scott's Bluff, Nebraska. Rebecca Burdick Winters, great-aunt of President Heber J. Grant's wife Augusta, died that day of cholera, and Ellis's father, as a friend of the family, volunteered to dig the grave. As Ellis held a lighted candle, he excavated the soil, buried "Sister Rebecca," and as a marker placed a wagon tire he had found by the wayside. Ellis still holding the candle, he chiseled onto the tire the legend, "Rebecca Winters, aged 50 years."

The Reynoldses were among the first settlers in Pleasant Grove, south of Salt Lake City, in Utah Valley, where Ellis's father acquired a farm.

Shy and introspective as a child, Ellis grew to be a self-confident and ambitious young girl, nurtured along by a loving and positive home atmosphere. She recalled in her memoirs that she could not remember hearing a cross word pass between her mother and father. Her deeply religious parents were not only kind, but did all they could to ensure that their children were comfortable and well-trained in useful skills. Ellis wrote:

> I was handy with my needle. I could sew and knit and do anything (I thought) that any woman else could do, thanks to a wise mother's early training when every day before I went to play I'd sew my seams and knit my rounds. Oh bless, Oh bless, her precious memory!

Ellis enjoyed school and work and was a vivacious and lively girl. She described her youth as "one endless day of sunshine" until January 28, 1861, when, during Ellis's fourteenth year, her mother died at the age of thirty-one. "I had never known grief," Ellis wrote. "It was my first real sorrow. I became sorrowful and moody. I was no more the gay and lighthearted girl I had ever been. I still went into society, but I did not join in the sports with my wonted alacrity, for every pleasure was fraught with a degree of sadness."

The death of her mother placed Ellis in the position of home-maker for her father, two sisters, and two brothers. To her fell the responsibility of cooking, washing, mending, and other general housework required to keep the household running smoothly while her father worked on their farm.

Ellis' experience of bearing such responsibility as a young teenager was not unique. Death was an ever-present reality during pioneer times, and most of her friends experienced the death of one of their parents while they were still living at home.

Not only did Ellis now shoulder the responsibility of caring for the family, but within a year of her mother's death, her father remarried. The result was an uncomfortable situation that soon drove Ellis to live with her grandparents in the tiny settlement of Battle Creek, south of Salt Lake City.

> . . . when my father took another wife . . . [it] was a very great trial for me as I was very young and did not look at things as I should have done. My father had been so very kind to me . . . and I was jealous that any other should take my place, not only mine, but my mother's. To see her take my mother's place in all things, have her chair at the table, and even be called by her name, was sometimes almost more than my jealous nature could bear.

Ellis, who yearned to socialize with her friends and to attend cultural events, soon became lonely and discontented living with her grandparents. She made occasional visits to Salt Lake City, attending musical and dramatic performances, going to General Conference, and visiting family friends and relatives.

One particular visit to "the city" marked a turning point in her life:

> I went to visit a friend of mine residing in the city—Lide Hybette, a niece of Clarissa Robison. The visit was one of great interest to me. I visited the theatre and saw Ora Lyne in the great play "Damon and Pythias." The first party I attended was in the Social Hall. The smooth and springy floor, delightful music, brilliant lights and the refinement I encountered on all sides was greatly in contrast with the rough floors, one violin, tallow candles and unpolished manners that I had always been accustomed to.

That evening, Ellis met and began receiving the romantic attentions of Zebulon Jacobs, through him becoming acquainted with his mother, Zina D. Jacobs Young, the wife of President Brigham Young. Ellis admitted that the warm attentions of the Young family were very flattering.

Shortly after Ellis returned to Pleasant Grove, President Young visited her hometown to preside over a church conference. Ellis, then seventeen, wrote of the occasion on which she first met the revered prophet and Church president:

> The [Church] meeting opened in a capacious bowery which had been erected for the occasion. The counsel and instruction given to the people were of the most exalting character. That day I saw the President watching me very closely. It was a puzzle to me. I could not understand why he should look at me so. I had never seen him except in the pulpit or some large assembly.
>
> In the evening there was [a] party. The evening was not far advanced when I had the honor of an introduction to President Young. He invited me to dance, but the floor was filled so quickly we had to wait till next time. Though many offered to give him their places he would not allow it; he took me to a seat and sat down by me. We conversed for some time. . . . I was almost astonished that I felt so much at ease in his presence, but his fatherly kindness almost entirely banished the timidity a person naturally feels in the presence of one who is so much her superior in wisdom and goodness. As we whirled through the mazy dance I felt that all eyes were upon us for it was not customary for the President to pay so much attention to persons outside of the family, although he was kind and cordial to all.

Ellis's lively intelligence must have made a favorable impression on President Young, for the next day he extended an invitation to her to come and live in the Beehive House with the Young family and attend school with his own children. Overwhelmed but eager for such a marvelous opportunity, Ellis accepted.

Ellis initially feared meeting the Young family ("my heart beat almost audibly") and expected to feel inferior. But she was warmly welcomed by children and adults alike and soon began to feel very much at home. Even at school, the other students were not as far advanced as she had expected. In fact, the teacher marked her recitation in grammar and compositions as "best."

Ellis accompanied President Young on several trips, knelt with the Young family in daily prayers, and sat in the president's box at the Salt Lake Theatre.

Ellis appreciated the opportunity President Young had provided for her to be privately tutored in the Beehive House, but her interests seemed to stray more toward her romantic involvements with several suitors. She was engaged briefly to "Zeb" Jacobs, but he and Ellis soon agreed to part, still good friends.

Ellis's fondest feelings were for Milford Bard Shipp, a gregarious, just-returned missionary whom she had known and admired for some time. She described him as

> . . . all that the enlivened fancy of girlhood or the matured judgment of woman could picture in her imagination. He was ambitious, ardent and energetic in all that was noble and laudable. Enthusiastic and spirited in conversation. In truth, I never saw a person who could so enchant and fascinate by the power of language.

President Young, however, was not so impressed. Eleven years Ellis's senior, Milford Shipp had been married twice before: one wife had died and the other had divorced him. President Young seemed to consider him somewhat of a drifter. But in the time Ellis spent with "Milf" and in the many private conversations they had, she felt she came to know his true "goodness and nobleness." She fell completely and unashamedly in love with him. Although President Young counseled her to use caution in her decision, he eventually gave his blessing to their marriage, as did Ellis's father.

Ellis and Milford were married May 5, 1866. Ellis was nineteen. The ceremony was performed by Heber C. Kimball in the Salt Lake Endowment House.

Ellis had dreamed that their marriage would be characterized by intellectual vigor and cultural refinement. But more practical matters soon intervened. The couple lived briefly in Fillmore, Utah, where Milford struggled to establish a new branch store with his father. The business failed and financial struggle followed, as did children, endless housekeeping tasks, and lonely months of separation while Milford served several missions for the Church.

For this idealistic and intelligent young woman, who was used to parties at the Beehive House and attendance at the Salt Lake Theatre, the daily routine of menial tasks soon brought frustration. Ellis dearly loved and cherished her children, but she lamented:

> I know that I am tired of this life of uselessness and unaccomplished desires, only so far as cooking, washing dishes and doing general housework goes. I believe that woman's life should not consist wholly and solely of routine duties.

She determined to keep her mind active and broaden her knowledge in a variety of subjects by establishing a daily routine of study and self-improvement. For the first nine years of her marriage, Ellis arose at 4 A.M. and studied for three solid hours before her household began to stir. Various diary entries indicate she studied poetry, history, English grammar, hygiene, and health. These daily study sessions served to improve her self-confidence and increase her persistence in learning more:

> May 3, 1871 [age 24]: I have risen early in the day for they are not sufficiently long for me to do all that I desire. The many practical duties that are mine preclude almost the possibility of intellectual study. I see by deducting a few golden moments from sleep, I may be able to add to my feeble stock of knowledge. Of late my desire for progress and improvement seems greater than ever before. I feel that gaining a deeper understanding of my inner nature—of its frailties and weaknesses—increases the desire to bring them into subjection.

Ellis continually felt her interest drawing toward the study of medicine. Sickness and death were grim realities among the early settlers of the West, and she herself had experienced personal losses because of inadequate medical care. This affectionate and loving young mother suffered through the deaths of five of her ten children, four of whom died in infancy. Ellis made a personal vow to do some day what she could to lower the high infant mortality rate.

That personal goal, however, did not seem even remotely possible until 1875, when her sister wife returned prematurely from the Women's Medical College in Philadelphia, homesick and lonely. Ellis decided to go in her place. With the support and encouragement of President Young and the Shipp family, Ellis, twenty-eight, left her three small children in the care of her three sister wives and boarded a train for Philadelphia to become a doctor.

Ellis studied under major financial difficulties, fought off continual health problems, and endured personal doubts about her ability to complete her degree. But she successfully passed her first year examinations and returned to Utah at the pleading of her husband to spend the summer with her family. She returned in the fall to Philadelphia, pregnant and with virtually no money. To earn her tuition, Ellis hired out as a dressmaker and, for a time, guarded the hall of cadavers at night, sleeping on a cot in the anteroom.

In the spring of the next year, still at school, Ellis gave birth to her sixth child, a girl. She spent the summer traveling through rural New Jersey with her infant, seeking sewing jobs to earn enough money to complete her schooling. She hired a girl to care for her baby while she finished her final year, and on March 14, 1878, Ellis Reynolds Shipp graduated with high honors, having earned the degree of Doctor of Medicine.

Upon her return to Utah, Ellis established her own practice, specializing in obstetrics, diseases of women, and minor surgery. She was the attending physician for more than five thousand births, including the delivery of the late Church leader Nathan Eldon Tanner. Ellis's fee for prenatal care and delivery was "$25 when it is convenient." She was often paid in produce—butter, eggs, or chickens. Her services also included ten visits to the home afterwards, when she would check on her patients' progress and help by performing other useful services such as changing the bed and cooking a meal.

Ellis was eager to share her knowledge. In 1879, she founded the School of Nursing and Obstetrics, in which she trained some five hundred women. The graduates of this school, who came from all over the West, took the regular territorial examination in obstetrics and became licensed midwives. One of these graduates was Olea Shipp, Ellis's daughter born in Philadelphia.

Some ten years after her graduation from medical school, Ellis returned to the East to become current on the new discovery that bacteria cause disease. Still later, in 1893, she spent a year in graduate study at the University of Michigan Medical School. As one of the best-educated physicians in Utah, Ellis was often sought out by male colleagues for advice.

Ellis Shipp's medical career spanned fifty years; she was still teaching obstetrics classes when in her eighties. Still high-spirited at age ninety-one, Ellis chided the women of Utah for showing such little interest in becoming physicians: "In a land renowned for its equal opportunities for women, it's simply amazing such a few follow a profession so befitting them."

Ellis deftly handled the challenge of combining a professional career with motherhood and homemaking. She helped each of her five surviving children through college: Milford Bard, Jr., a physician, from Jefferson Medical College, Philadelphia; Olea from the School of Music, Ann Arbor, Michigan; Richard, an attorney, from Harvard University; Ellis from Columbia University with a master's degree; and Nellie from the University of Utah. Even more important to Ellis was her knowledge that each of her children was a person of integrity who shared her religious faith.

In addition to being a doctor and a mother, Ellis remained a devoted member of the Church. She served for many years as a member of the general boards of the Relief Society and the Young Women's Mutual Improvement Association. She was also president of the Utah Women's Press Club and a delegate to the National Council of Women at Washington, D.C.

Dr. Ellis Reynolds Shipp died quietly in Salt Lake City, January 31, 1939, at the age of ninety-two. She had played an important role in the improvement of medical care in the Great Basin, contributing greatly to the health and well-being of thousands of her fellow Latter-day Saints. In her later years, Ellis mused, "Had I fully realized the magnitude of the undertaking, I would have shrunk from it."

In his book, *Of Medicine, Hospitals, and Doctors,* Dr. Ralph T. Richards wrote: "No one did more toward solving this problem [medical care for women in the pioneer West] than Dr. Ellis R. Shipp, 'Utah's Grand Old Lady,' unquestionably the outstanding woman of her time."

16

Annie Wells Cannon

Versatile and Exemplary Leader

The completion of the transcontinental railroad in 1869 brought many changes to the Saints in the Great Basin. Not only did it provide easier transportation for those traveling to and from Utah, but it also brought temptations to the Mormon sisters in the form of new tastes and fashions.

President Brigham Young cringed as he saw sisters walking the streets of Salt Lake City wearing the Grecian Bend, a dress style popular at the time featuring long, flowing skirts and mutton-legged sleeves. The Grecian Bend, President Young said, gave women a hump on their backs that made them look like camels; mutton-legged sleeves "took seven yards for the sleeves, and three for the dress"; and long trains would drag up the dirt, raise dust, and waste many yards of cloth. He admonished the sisters to use their means to make contributions to such worthy causes as the transportation of the "pure in heart" from abroad, rather than waste their money on "useless articles that do no good to the body of the persons who use them."

Seeing the need to take stronger action to curtail the increasing "worldliness" of the sisters, President Young called his many wives and daughters together one cool autumn evening in 1869 in the parlor of his home, the Lion House, in Salt Lake City. He counseled them in economy and modest living and expressed his desire to bring about reform in the community, with his own daughters setting the example.

The Young family voted its support, and under the direction of Eliza R. Snow, the "Young Ladies' Department of the Co-operative Retrenchment Association" was formed. Within a few months, several score Retrenchment Societies had blossomed throughout the region.

One young woman who benefited greatly from participation in the newly created organization was Elizabeth Anne Wells, always referred to as "Annie." Born in a two-story adobe house on State Street in downtown Salt Lake City on December 7, 1859, Annie became active in the Retrenchment Society of the Salt Lake Thirteenth Ward at the age of thirteen.

Along with instructions on how to "retrench" from worldly ways, Annie was taught many skills in the Society to increase her self-sufficiency. She learned to piece quilts, crochet, make hats, knit stockings, and glean wheat. Social and cultural activities were a regular part of Society activity; Annie and her young friends enjoyed molasses candy pulls, corn-husking bees, sing-alongs, and winter sleigh riding. A favorite activity among the youth was always dancing, although Minerva Knowlton, who grew up in Grantsville, recorded in her memoirs that her ward questioned the propriety of certain dances and they eventually "voted to abstain from waltzing."

Both of Annie's parents held important leadership positions in the Church. Her father, Daniel H. Wells, distinguished himself in public service. As a nonmember, he befriended the Saints during the harsh persecutions in Nauvoo and he very inexpensively sold them the land on which the Nauvoo Temple was eventually built. Daniel was finally baptized in 1846 and crossed the Great Plains with the pioneers to the Salt Lake Valley in 1848. Before his death in 1891 he had served as superintendent of Church public works, commander of the Nauvoo Legion, Salt Lake City mayor, president of the Manti Temple, and counselor to President Brigham Young.

Annie's mother was the well-known Emmeline B. Wells, editor of the *Woman's Exponent* for thirty-seven years and fifth general president of the Relief Society. Active all her life in Church organizations, Emmeline was also a vocal advocate of women's rights. Her editorials for the *Exponent* covered a broad range of women's issues— equal pay for equal work, women's voting rights, even equality in athletic programs. In 1879 and 1882, Emmeline and her close friend Zina D. H. Young attended conventions of the National Women's Suffrage Association, delivering papers on Mormon life in Utah and petitioning Congress to recognize the rights of the children of plural marriages.

Since Annie's father was rarely home, Emmeline became the major force in the lives of Annie and her three sisters, each of whom had a close and mutually supportive relationship with their mother. As she sat sewing and mending, Emmeline taught the girls songs and poems. By the time Annie started to school she could recite "Twenty Years Ago," "Bingen on the Rhine," "The Blackberry Girl," "Proud Charlotte," and other pretty poems and ballads. She could even recite "Lochinvar's Ride" from Sir Walter Scott's *Marmion*—a long ballad which tells of a young woman (Ellen) about to be married to "a laggard in love and a dastard in war." At the wedding feast the brave Lochinvar appears, claims a dance with Ellen, and, when they reach the hall door, swings Ellen onto his horse and rides off with her into the sunset, the two living happily ever after. Annie also learned to sing such songs as "Forget-me-not," "Billy Boy," and "The Hen with Ten Chicks." The teacher was amazed that little Annie had learned so much and wanted to borrow the books from which she had memorized these selections, only to find out that they were in her mother's head!

Needless to say, Annie and her sisters also learned to sew—rows upon rows of fine tucking for the shirt bosoms of the men in the family, tucks and ruffles for baby clothes to give to neighbors, and pillow cases, petticoats, and dresses. They also learned how to cook—baked beans, doughnuts, apple fritters, and minute pudding. So Annie was well prepared by her mother to carry out the objectives of retrenchment.

But, above all, Annie was a little organizer. In this respect her work with the Retrenchment Society was only the beginning. She organized girl's clubs, musical and dramatic groups, literary societies, and study groups. She joined with others in studying the scriptures as well as literary works; indeed, she read the New Testament when she was only ten. She had almost perfect attendance in Sunday School, once wading through deep snow to find only one member of the superintendency who had likewise braved the storm. When she was fifteen, she joined with several hundred other Sunday School girls to welcome President Ulysses S. Grant as he rode through the streets of Salt Lake City in 1875, the first president to visit the territory. Dressed in white, with wreaths of flowers on their heads and waving flags in their hands, they made an indelible impression on the president.

Annie received her early education in the Salt Lake City schools, later attending the private school of Miss Mary E. Cook, held in the Social Hall. She graduated in 1879 from the University of Deseret, where she took a liberal-arts course.

Of the four girls born to Emmeline and Daniel H. Wells, Annie was said to have been most like her mother. She loved books and read voraciously. She was considered somewhat of an intellectual, a lover of ideas and learning. Seeing and assisting Emmeline in her various causes served to prepare Annie for a life of similar service. She sat with her mother for many hours, helping to write and prepare material for the *Woman's Exponent*.

Annie's three sisters, Mellie (Melanie), Emmie (Emily), and Louie (Louise), were talented and artistically inclined. Their mother loved the evenings the girls spent at home entertaining friends with singing and playing. The Wasatch Literary Club, to which many of Salt Lake's early intellectuals belonged, was organized in her home. This was a forerunner of the Mutual Improvement Associations of the Church. Many entries in Emmeline's diary make some mention of the girls' activities, expressing many worries over their pursuits, social lives, loves, and illnesses. It was a tragic loss to Annie when two of her sisters died unexpectedly in their twenties.

On July 24, 1879, when Annie was nineteen, the annual Sunday School Jubilee was held in the big tabernacle on Temple Square in Salt Lake City. These were the equivalent of general conferences for young people—songs, talks, recitations, original dramas, and other interesting highlights. Nicely dressed in a new black grenadine dress and lovely black "picture" hat, fair-skinned Annie, with her honey-blonde hair, must have made a striking appearance. Accompanying her mother to the special seats for the press, Annie was seated next to John Q. Cannon, son of Elder George Q. Cannon of the Quorum of the Twelve Apostles. John was at the time a reporter for the *Deseret News*. It is doubtful that John and Annie remembered much about the program—they laughed a good deal, talked in hushed tones about things that young people talk about, and when the program was over, John walked Annie home. They began to see each other almost daily, were engaged by the end of the year, and were married the following March, when Annie was twenty.

Shortly after their marriage, in a practice fairly common at the time, John was called on a mission to Europe. Several months later, when John was called to preside over the Swiss-German Mission, Annie was able to join him. Her letters home, published in the *Exponent*, give a vivid account of visits to the art galleries, museums, operas, and other cultural and architectural attractions in the great cities of Europe.

Annie and John eventually had twelve children (one died as an infant); Annie frequently won the local award for having the largest family as well as receiving special recognition for being the mother of a set of twins. Of her children, one was a diplomat, one a nationally-recognized social worker, and another legal advisor for the Civil Service Commission in Washington, D.C.

But that does not end Annie's story. Annie had been active in the Relief Society for many years before her marriage. In fact, she was only fourteen when her name first appeared on the roll of the organization. One can imagine that Emmeline was eager for her young daughter to become involved as early as possible in this women's organization which had played such an important role in the history of the Church and in the settlement of the Great Basin. While still a young woman, Annie was for sixteen years president of the Pioneer Stake Relief Society in Salt Lake City—a stake that included eleven wards and branches. Besides performing her executive duties, she spent much of her time working with the poor and those who were ill. To help with this work she established a large emergency cabinet, including what was known as a maternity bundle—the first of its kind in Relief Society—fitted out with medical and other supplies: sheets and quilts, nightgown, syringes, bedpans, hot water bottles, layettes for babies, and so forth. There were also burial clothes and temple outfits. This was a pattern for many hundreds which were later established by other wards and stakes.

When she was forty-two Annie was appointed a member of the Relief Society General Board, a position she held from 1902-1910 and again from 1919-1939, a total of twenty-eight years.

Annie used her ability to write throughout her life. She was a frequent contributor of both prose and poetry to the *Woman's Exponent* and the *Relief Society Magazine* and, when in Europe, in her twenties, she wrote a brief history of the Relief Society which was translated into several languages for the benefit of the sisters in various nations. Her numerous articles treated domestic arts, family life, and women and politics. During one period she contributed a series of articles under the title "Passing Thoughts" and signed them "Camelia," a pseudonym she used at the time. For fifteen years she was associate editor of the *Exponent* and, later, when her husband became editor of the *Deseret News,* she was his dedicated assistant.

It was at Annie's suggestion that the Relief Society Board published a 1942 volume entitled *Our Legacy: The Relief Society Anthology of Verse and Prose.* Published during the centennial year of the Relief Society, the volume contained 328 poems written by Latter-day Saint women, including several poems by Annie.

Among Annie's other pioneering projects were the founding of one of the first Relief Society stake libraries, the writing and publication of the first Relief Society Handbook for leaders of that organization, and the establishment of the first Red Cross chapter in Utah under the direction of Clara Barton. Annie became the first president of the Utah War Mothers organization, a group of women whose sons had fought in World War I. She also served as state president of its successor organization, the Service Star Legion. Three of Annie's sons were in World War I—one in the Army, one in the Navy, and one in the Marines. Annie was also Utah's Chairman of the European Relief Council, which raised money for the relief of starving children in Central and Southern Europe after World War I. She was also Utah Director of the American Relief Administration, American Flag Day Association, and American Women's Association. She was a charter member and later president of the Daughters of the Utah Pioneers, and for many years chairman of the children's department of the Salt Lake County Library.

Annie followed the politically active footsteps of her mother. At the age of twenty she was an elected delegate to the city convention of her party—the only woman so elected. After the turn of the century she was elected to the Utah House of Representatives, where she was largely responsible for the passage of four important measures in the interest of women: a minimum wage law for women, a dependent mothers' pension law, a bill providing for the equal guardianship of children, and a law creating the office of a woman deputy in the personnel department. She also sponsored a bill providing for the establishment of a girls' dormitory at the University of Utah. That she took her job in the legislature seriously is evidenced by the fact that she was present to answer every roll call.

Annie Wells Cannon died September 2, 1942, at the age of eighty-two. At her funeral in Salt Lake City, David O. McKay, then an Apostle, said: "Her life and accomplishments have been little short of miraculous."

Thomas Romney wrote:

> Seldom can there be found in one woman so many outstanding and ennobling qualities of such wide diversity as those possessed by Annie Wells Cannon. She was highly intellectual, having the ability to grasp intricate problems in the metaphysical world; and equally well could she solve the complexities arising in the field of domestic economy. She was equally at home with the highly educated and with those of limited opportunities. Her editorials sparked with brilliance, and her civic and ecclesiastical contributions marked her as a woman of sound judgment, unbounded energy and splendid vision.

Annie's relationship with her mother and her membership in the Retrenchment Association and Relief Society combined to train her in her early years to be of service to her family and the Church, as well as to her community. Those who knew Annie intimately knew her to be an excellent homemaker as well as a devoted wife and mother.

17

Mary Elizabeth Woolley Chamberlain
From Milkmaid to Mayor

Eleven-year-old Mamie Woolley could hardly believe what her father was asking her to do. Edwin D. Woolley lifted his daughter on top of a large load of hay, handed her the reins, and gave her instructions to drive the team a distance of six miles to their farm in St. George. The trip would take Mamie over dusty range land, "chucky" wagon roads, and through the Virgin River "which was full of quick-sand—and really dangerous," she recalled. "My heart was in my mouth till I was safely over it." Edwin drove another team ahead of his daughter, frequently checking on her progress. They both arrived home after dark with Mamie exhausted but feeling quite like "a hero."

That day was typical of the experiences Mamie Woolley faced as a young girl growing up on a ranch in southern Utah. Born on January 31, 1870, in St. George, she was named Mary Elizabeth after her two grandmothers, but was quickly nicknamed "Mame" or "Mamie." She was the second of the ten children born to Edwin Dilworth Woolley, Jr., and Emma Geneva Bentley.

Mamie grew up as what she later called "a very plain and unattractive child, large for my years." She was the butt of jokes because of her big feet, and suffered from her mother's homemade remedies for childhood diseases:

Mother always saved the inner lining of a chicken's gizzard, dried it, then powdered it and mixed with equal parts of sugar and used it for indigestion. A live frog was split down the belly and placed on the throat for putrid sore throat (now diphtheria). Lobelia emetic was used for almost any and every complaint. Oh! What an ordeal to go through! Both for the patient and nurse, for Mother always insisted that we vomit at least three times before she relaxed her efforts.

When Mamie was eleven, her older sister, Minnie, died of diphtheria. This left Mamie, now the oldest child, to shoulder much of the responsibility for helping her parents with the endless routine of work at home and on the farm.

Mamie claimed that her father had always wished she had been a boy. At least he seemed to make no distinction between the jobs he gave her to do and the ones usually assigned to young men. The result was a young girl who gained confidence in her ability to accomplish almost anything, including various jobs usually tackled by men.

Mamie's confidence began to grow during her early years as a milkmaid. She was only twelve when her father was assigned by Mormon Apostle Erastus Snow to look after the Church's ranch in Kanab, Kane County, Utah. On the ranch each summer were more than one hundred cows which had calved—beef cows to be sure, but nevertheless cows which produced milk. Her father chose a group of boys and girls, Mamie among them, to do the milking and to make butter and cheese. She had to be up as soon as it was light so the task could be done before the flies became a bother and the sun got too hot. The young men wore blue overalls and heavy shirts, while the girls wore big, sack aprons made of blue denim over their dresses and red bandannas to cover their hair. The milk was poured into a large vat in the cheese room. Twelve-year-old Mamie wrote, "I milked an average of twenty cows night and morning every summer as long as we ran the dairy."

When Mamie and the other children saw a resemblance between the cow and the facial expression, size, voice, or disposition of a certain person, they would give the cow that person's name. Visitors were often amused to hear the children call out names such as "Napoleon" and "Madame Patti" while they worked with the cows; many of their neighbors and friends in St. George were duly honored with a bovine namesake.

When Mamie finished her work on the farm, there was plenty for her to do inside the house. "Besides milking cows night and morning," she wrote, "I had to cook and do the housework, including the washing for the family and several hired men. Mother was in a delicate condition and could do very little except supervise."

The end of the day brought pleasant socializing. Mamie wrote: "In the evenings after milking and other chores were done we would gather in the little log cabin . . . and listen to Aunt Mishie sing and play on the little old organ." Mamie remembered hearing "Ben Bolt," "When You and I Were Young, Maggie," "The Bridge," "Silver Threads Among the Gold," "The Spanish Cavalier," "The Gypsy's Warning," "Tenting Tonight," "My Bonnie Lies over the Ocean," and many Sunday School hymns.

Mamie's parents lived by the motto of "Strict Economy and Unceasing Industry" and trained their children to do the same. Mamie was not yet ten years old before she learned techniques for making molasses, butter, jams and jellies, tallow candles, soap, and home-cured vinegar. She plucked feathers from the family's flock of ducks and used them to make large, fluffy down pillows. She wove homemade carpets from well-worn clothing and braided thick rugs out of men's overalls, overcoats, and other heavy materials.

Mamie recalled the beds she and her family made and slept on:

> Our beds were usually heavy ticks, filled with nice clean straw, wild hay, or corn husks, filled fresh every fall, stuffed till they were almost round and so high when placed on the bedstead that we needed a step-ladder to get into them. On my sixteenth birthday Father gave me a lovely featherbed, and I do not think a queen was ever prouder of a possession.

Mamie made a specialty of knitting striped cashmere stockings. Whenever she had an hour of leisure time, she could be found sitting in the shade of an oak tree knitting as many rows as time permitted. The white or gray yarn was bought at the Orderville United Order factory and then dyed a variety of colors. Mamie often engaged in "knitting races" with her friends, the "Seegmiller girls," and became quite expert. She did not own a pair of store-bought stockings until she was past twenty, and she was over fifty before she had a pair of silk hose. The speed with which she must have been able to knit is evident in the fact that during World War I (1914-1918) she knit a pair of men's socks each day for weeks, in addition to earning a living, doing her own housework, and tending her children and garden.

In the early days the Woolley family worked hard to keep everyone fed and clothed and usually spent little time or money on anything that was not a necessity. While they were still living in St. George, however, Mamie's father made a valiant effort to give her a chance to study music. They lived near a Sister DeFreize, an Englishwoman, who gave organ lessons, and Edwin promised to buy Mamie her own organ as soon as she learned to play a tune. The young milkmaid wrote how she felt sitting down in front of the ivory keys for her first lessons:

> I had music in my soul but it was hard to get it into my fingers, as they were used only to sweeping, scrubbing, washing, milking cows, etc., and they were not lady fingers to begin with. So it was quite a task and required almost more patience than I could muster.

Mamie persisted, however, and soon wrote to her father that she could now play "The Corn Flower Waltz" and "Nearer My God To Thee." Edwin was thrilled and immediately ordered a Kimball organ, which was soon delivered to their home in St. George. Mamie was now able to show off her talent for the family, but described later the problems of practicing at home:

> [My practising] practically ended there, as there was always so much work to do. Mother offered to do all the work if I would only practice; but she was not strong and could not do half that needed doing, and when she sent me in the front room to practice for an hour, I would find the organ covered with dust and the children's clothing, playthings, etc., scattered over the floor and I could not sit down to practice till the room was set to rights, dusted, etc., and by that time the hour was up and I was called to other tasks. Thus it went day after day till I finally forgot what little I knew.

Mamie occasionally went to school during the winters and told of experiences there that proved she was lively, full of energy, and often outspoken. On one occasion, when she was fifteen, Principal Henry E. Bowman asked for the name and age of each student. When it came her turn, Mamie shouted out, "Sweet sixteen and never been kissed!" The students roared with laughter and she was teased by her classmates about the remark for years to come.

That same school year, Mamie was courted by her first beau, Abia E. Johnson. They "kept company" all winter, with Abia often arriving to visit her before she finished her work. On such occasions, Mamie's younger brothers, Jode and Roy, would entertain him, often telling Abia how their sister cleaned and swept extra thoroughly on the days she knew he was coming. Younger brothers could be a nuisance to lovers in pioneer days too, and Mamie recalled:

> One evening we were sitting cosily in the front room when Roy, age eight, came in swinging the 'lariat,' stating that he was going to lasso Abia's nose, much to the latter's embarrassment, as it was a very prominent feature.

When Mamie was nineteen, her father sold his interest in the Upper Kanab Ranch where they had lived for many years and bought a home in Lower Kanab, a location which afforded better schooling for the growing children, offered more social advantages, and placed Edwin closer to his duties as the newly appointed stake president. He took Mamie with him to Salt Lake City to select furniture for the new home. They shipped it to Salina, Sevier County, the end of the railroad line, and then freighted it by wagon from there—an eight-day trip. There were two big wagonloads of furniture, both stacked high. Mamie, ever her father's helper, drove one wagon and her father the other. They camped out every night and slept on the ground. Mamie hitched and unhitched the teams, curried the horses, and fed and watered her own team.

Among the new-fangled luxuries the Woolley family enjoyed in their new home was their first indoor, built-in bathtub. Water had to be carried in by bucket and poured in, but could run out through the drain. A little ditch sent the water to the trees and flowers on their lot. Mamie wrote:

> . . . many are the weary and travel-stained apostles, senators, governors, drummers, and others who enjoyed a refreshing bath, as that was about the first thing Mother suggested when anyone arrived, and they were always surprised and delighted to enjoy such a treat as they found very few such along the route.

Mamie found it difficult to be the daughter of a stake president. Everything she and her sisters did was carefully observed by the community and often criticized. "Other girls could say and do things out of the way and no notice was ever taken of it," she complained. "But let one of us side-step the least bit and the whole town knew about it!"

When bloomers and divided skirts first became popular, Mamie was the first to don them while riding horseback and was criticized for being "so unwomanly." Following one such ride through town, she recorded:

> Old Brother Charles Cram appeared before the stake presidency at one of their council meetings with a complaint that "Mamie" Woolley had disgraced the town. They all gasped and wondered whatever was coming, and when told to proceed, he said, "Well sir, she rode down the streets of Kanab, Sir, straddle of a hoss, looking like a spread eagle, Sir!!" They all gave a sigh of relief, and a hearty laugh, and told him he had just woke from a Rip Van Winkle sleep.

Mamie showed little interest in school until 1890, when she attended the Latter-day Saints College in Salt Lake City for one year, taking the "normal" or teacher's course. She acted in plays, gave recitations, benefited from weekend trips to the canyons with other girls, and attended frequent socials. In the commencement exercises she was chosen to represent the women students. Among other things, she made the following remark in her talk:

> The young ladies of this institution (I am proud to say) stand on an equal plane with the young men and receive from them the respect which equals demand. Sex with us is no distinction. If there is anything to be performed and a lady is capable, the fact of her being "fair" does not deter her. Her opinion is expressed and sanctioned, her testimony borne and sustained the same as that of her brethren.

Despite the fact that she had trained to be a teacher, Mamie returned to St. George to become a clerk in the "Bowman and Company" general store, earning $30 per month. This was the first money Mamie had ever earned and she was very proud. It is interesting to note what she purchased the first time she bought anything with her own money: a gold pocket watch, which cost $62.50, and a load of hay at $25.00 per ton for her riding horse, "Gazelle." While working at the store, Mamie again showed her versatility. One minute she was cutting a slab of greasy bacon, the next she was measuring ten yards of dainty fine lace or ribbon. Then she would do down into the cellar for a dozen horseshoe nails and a hundred pounds of oats, and follow by climbing the stairs to measure silks and satins. She wrote: "There were no departments with a special clerk for each, nor was I detailed to wait on 'ladies only,' but did whatever was to be done."

Mamie became well acquainted with the members of the community through the general store. After Utah became a state in 1896, when she was twenty-six and still single, she was elected county clerk—making her the first woman county clerk in Utah.

> I knew [she wrote] the financial rating of every man in the county from the amount of taxes he paid, and could judge pretty well of his honesty by the way he met his obligations and paid his debts. I was also in a position to know the ecclesiastical standing of every member of the church in the county from the amount of tithing they paid. After the tithing records were made out by the bishops of each ward, and all compiled by the stake clerk, I had the task of copying every one of them by hand, before they were sent to the Presiding Bishopric's Office in Salt Lake City.

Mamie soon knew every man, woman, and child over four years of age in the county by their given names. Likewise, everyone knew and liked her. In November of 1911, in a history-making election, Mamie was chosen president of the town board or mayor of Kanab, an office she held for two years. She was the second woman to be elected mayor of any city in the United States. The entire board was composed of women, a fact which was also unprecedented. Mamie wrote of it:

> Our election was intended as a joke and no one thought seriously of it at the time. When the election day dawned, there was no ticket in the field; no one seemed interested in the supervision of the town, so the loafers on the ditchbank (of which there were always plenty) proceeded to make up a ticket (of women) as a burlesque. But there was no other ticket in opposition, so, of course, we were elected. When Father came and told me about it, I was disgusted and said I would not think of qualifying and I knew others would not even if I did, but he insisted that we take it seriously and put the job over as he knew we could, and he would give us all the support and backing possible. (Others indicated their support). . . . So, after due consideration and much debating, we decided to tackle the job and see what we could do.

Joke or not, they gave Kanab what many oldtimers later said was the best government they ever had. Under Mamie's leadership, the city placed a tax on peddlers who came through, thus giving support to local merchants; purchased lumber and built a dike to protect homes and property from the floods that menaced the town from the time it was built; gave prizes for the cleanest streets and sidewalks around any home; discontinued ball games and horse races on Sunday; prohibited gambling and games of chance; passed a liquor ordinance; and prohibited the shooting of robins and other songbirds within the city limits.

Eleven years prior to her election as mayor, Mamie had married Thomas Chamberlain of Orderville, and had given birth to their two sons, Royal in 1902 and Edwin Dilworth ("Dee") in 1905. So, in addition to the service she rendered to the community, Mamie did all her own housework, cared for her children, and made her own "carpets, rugs, quilts, soap and all other things that pioneer women have to do."

While Mamie continued to clerk at Bowman's general store, she bottled fruit, made preserves, pickles, and dried corn, served as superintendent of her ward religion class, and taught a Sunday School class.

After her husband's death in 1918, Mamie was left to support herself and her two young sons. To do this, she baked as many as thirty loaves of bread a day for several years and sold them to Grand Canyon tourists who came through Kanab. She also sold, by consignment, a line of women's hats, and took in boarders. When she and her two sons moved to Provo in 1922, Mamie canvassed the town door-to-door selling silk underwear for the "Shaughnessy Knitting Company."

After both her sons were married, Mamie moved to Salt Lake City, where she lived the rest of her life, serving as an ordinance worker in the Salt Lake Temple. In her later years, Mamie enjoyed traveling throughout the country to places of interest and visiting her children, grandchildren, and friends.

Mamie Woolley Chamberlain died in 1953 at the age of 83. At her funeral, she was eulogized as a "wise counselor, warm friend," and "an example of thrift, industry and cheerfulness." A step-daughter, Elsie Chamberlain Carroll, praised her efforts to stay "intellectually alive" by taking courses at Brigham Young University and attending various concerts and lectures. Perhaps the most heartwarming picture of this charming, fun-loving woman was painted by a granddaughter,

Renee Chamberlain Dyer, who recalled how her Grandmother Chamberlain "loved to make me laugh by taking out her false teeth and 'scaring' me with them."

Mamie is buried in Kanab, not far from the ranch she milked cows on and the city offices where she served as mayor.

Bibliographical Note

Index

Bibliographical Note

The basic historical narrative upon which we have depended for setting and for general information is James B. Allen and Glen M. Leonard, *The Story of the Latter-day Saints* (Salt Lake City: Deseret Book Company, 1976). Contemporary biographical sources include: Edward W. Tullidge, *The Women of Mormondom* (New York, 1877); Augusta Joyce Crocheron, *Representative Women of Deseret: A Book of Biographical Sketches* (Salt Lake City, 1884); and Andrew Jenson, *Latter-day Saint Biographical Encyclopedia*, 4 vols. (Salt Lake City: Andrew Jenson History Company, 1901-36). More recent biographical sources which have been particularly helpful are: Vicky Burgess-Olson, ed., *Sister Saints* (Provo, Utah: Brigham Young University Press, 1978); Claudia L. Bushman, ed., *Mormon Sisters: Women in Early Utah* (Cambridge, Mass.: Emmeline Press Limited, 1976); Kenneth W. Godfrey, Audrey M. Godfrey, and Jill Mulvay Derr, *Women's Voices: An Untold History of the Latter-day Saints, 1830-1900* (Salt Lake City: Deseret Book Company, 1982); and Richard Van Wagoner and Steve Walker, *A Book of Mormons* (Salt Lake City: Signature Books, 1982).

Except where indicated, all unpublished manuscripts are located in the Library-Archives of the Historical Department of The Church of Jesus Christ of Latter-day Saints, 50 East North Temple Street, Salt Lake City, Utah. Our task was rendered incomparably easier by Davis Bitton's *Guide to Mormon Diaries and Autobiographies* (Provo: Brigham Young University Press, 1977).

Introduction. This essay is similar to Leonard J. Arrington, "LDS Girls in the Pioneer West," *New Era* 12 (July 1982):16-22. We are grateful for permission to use portions of it here. See also Leonard Arrington, "Blessed Damozels: Women in Mormon History," *Dialogue* 6 (Summer 1971):22-31; and "Persons for All Seasons: Women in Mormon History," *BYU Studies* 20 (Fall 1979):39-58.

Chapter 1. Papers of Mary Elizabeth Rollins Lightner, LDS Church Archives. These include a diary she kept in 1863; an autobiography she wrote in 1887; a typescript of a testimony she gave in 1902; a signed testimony she gave at Brigham Young University in 1905; a typewritten biography by her granddaughter Elsie E. Barrett; and some letters from and to her. Also "Mary Elizabeth Rollins Lightner," *Utah Genealogical and Historical Magazine* 17 (July-October 1926):193-205, 250-60; "Mary Elizabeth Rollins Lightner," in Kate B. Carter, ed., *Our Pioneer Heritage*, 20 vols. (Salt Lake City: Daughters of the Utah Pioneers, 1958-77), 5:305-24; N. B. Lundwall, comp., *The Life and Testimony of Mary E. Lightner* (n.p., n.d.), LDS Church Archives.

Chapter 2. We have used *Biography of Elizabeth Haven Barlow*, republished by the Israel Barlow Family Association (Salt Lake City [?], July 1958);

and "Mother of Eight," in Carter, *Our Pioneer Heritage*, 19:318-34. The latter is Sister Barlow's autobiography. We have also inspected the minutes of the Nauvoo Female Relief Society, 1842-1844.

Chapter 3. The basic source for this chapter is "Firm in the Faith: Drusilla Dorris Hendricks," in Carter, *Our Pioneer Heritage*, 20:241-72. The typescript on which this was based is in the LDS Church Archives.

Chapter 4. Jane Snyder Richards, "Reminiscences of Mrs. F. D. Richards," 1880, MS., Bancroft Library, Berkeley, California, P-F 4; Orson F. Whitney, *History of Utah*, 4 vols. (Salt Lake City: George Q. Cannon & Sons, 1892-1904), 4:581; Connie Duncan Cannon, "Jane Snyder Richards: The Blue-White Diamond," in Vicky Burgess-Olson, ed., *Sister Saints* (Provo, Utah: Brigham Young University Press, 1978), pp. 173-98; various documents in the "Jane S. Richards File," LDS Church Archives.

Chapter 5. "Journal of Rachel Emma Woolley Simmons," in Kate B. Carter, ed., *Heart Throbs of the West*, 12 vols. (Salt Lake City: Daughters of the Utah Pioneers, 1936-51), 11:153-208; Leonard J. Arrington, *From Quaker to Latter-day Saint: Bishop Edwin D. Woolley* (Salt Lake City: Deseret Book Company, 1976).

Chapter 6. Diary of Patience Loader Rozsa Archer in LDS Church Archives; Godfrey, Godfrey, and Derr, *Women's Voices*, esp. pp. 222-42; Rebecca Cornwall and Leonard J. Arrington, *Rescue of the 1856 Handcart Companies* (Provo, Utah: Charles Redd Center, 1981); interview with Drusilla Loader Smith of Pleasant Grove, Utah, a grandniece, 31 January 1983.

Chapter 7. Various documents in the file of Anna Widtsoe in the LDS Church Archives; John A. Widtsoe, *In the Gospel Net: The Story of Anna Karine Gaarden Widtsoe* (Salt Lake City: An Improvement Era Book, 1942).

Chapter 8. Based primarily on "Journal of Minnie Petersen Brown," in Kate B. Carter, ed., *Treasures of Pioneer History*, 6 vols. (Salt Lake City: Daughters of the Utah Pioneers, 1952-58), 4:297-348.

Chapter 9. Louise Degn, "Susanna Goudin Cardon: An Italian Convert to Mormonism," in Burgess-Olson, *Sister Saints*, pp. 119-36; Leonard J. Arrington, "The Economic Role of Pioneer Mormon Women," *Western Humanities Review* 9 (Spring 1955):145-64; "Susanna Goudin Cardon," by her granddaughter, Rebecca Cardon Hickman Peterson, typescript, LDS Church Archives; Carl W. Arrington, "Waldensian Immigrants in Cache Valley, Utah," typescript generously furnished by the author; Archibald F. Bennett, "The Vaudois Revisited," *Improvement Era* 51 (January 1948):12-14, 56-58; interview with Margaret Cardon Hickman, a granddaughter, Logan, Utah, 2 April 1982; interview with Sybil Kenner, a granddaughter, Logan, Utah, 3 April 1982.

Chapter 10. Margery W. Ward, ed., *A Fragment: The Autobiography of Mary Jane Mount Tanner* (Salt Lake City: University of Utah Library, 1980); "Mary Jane Mount Tanner," in Godfrey, Godfrey, and Derr, *Women's Voices,* pp. 307-24. Manuscript copy and typewritten copies of the autobiography are in the LDS Church Archives.

Chapter 11. Nelle Spilsbury Hatch, *Mother Jane's Story* (Wasco, Calif.: Shafer Publishing Co., c. 1964), esp. "Aunt Louise," pp. 39-54; "The Story of Sariah Louisa Chamberlain Redd," as told by Jane Redd Spilsbury to her daughter Nelle Spilsbury Hatch, typescript, LDS Church Archives; Amasa Jay Redd, ed., *Lemuel Hardison Redd, Jr., 1856-1923: Pioneer, Leader, Builder* (Salt Lake City: Privately published, 1967); Leonard J. Arrington and Davis Bitton, "Lemuel H. Redd: Down the Chute to San Juan," in *Saints Without Halos: The Human Side of Mormon History* (Salt Lake City: Signature Books, 1981), pp. 90-95.

Chapter 12. Autobiography of Sarah Endiaetta Young Vance, typescript, LDS Church Archives; Keith Calvin Terry, "The Contribution of Medical Women During the First Fifty Years in Utah" (Master's thesis, Brigham Young University, 1964); Roberta Flake Clayton, *Pioneer Women of Arizona* (Mesa, Ariz., 1969).

Chapter 13. Catherine Heggie Griffiths, "A Story of the Life of Catherine H. Griffiths," MS., Special Collections, Utah State University Library; interview with Sylvia G. Loosle, daughter of Catherine H. Griffiths, 10 April 1982; Joel E. Ricks, ed., *The History of a Valley: Cache Valley, Utah-Idaho* (Logan, Utah: Cache Valley Centennial Commission, 1956); Carol Cornwall Madsen, "A Survey of the Life of Cache Valley Women in 1890," typescript, prepared for the Ronald V. Jensen Living Historical Farm, Logan, Utah, 1979.

Chapter 14. Carol Cornwall Madsen, "Louisa Lula Greene Richards: 'Remember the Women of Zion,' " in Burgess-Olson, *Sister Saints,* pp. 433-53; interview with Helen Richards Gardner, a granddaughter, Logan, Utah, 23 January 1983; "Lula Greene Richards," *Juvenile Instructor* 66 (March 1931):267-69; Leonard J. Arrington, "Louisa Lula Greene Richards: Woman Journalist of the Early West, *Improvement Era* 72 (May 1969):28-32; "Louisa L. Greene Richards," *Young Woman's Journal,* December 1891, pp. 97-99; Diary of Lula Greene Richards, MS., LDS Church Archives.

Chapter 15. Ellis Shipp Musser, ed., *The Early Autobiography and Diary of Ellis Reynolds Shipp, M.D.,* (Salt Lake City [?]: Privately published, 1962); Gail Farr Casterline, "Dr. Ellis Reynolds Shipp: Pioneer Utah Physician," in Burgess-Olson, *Sister Saints,* pp. 363-81; Judy Skalla, "Beloved Healer," in The Western Writers of America, *The Women Who Made the West* (New York: Doubleday & Co., 1980), pp. 152-63.

Chapter 16. Leonard J. Arrington, "The Economic Role of Pioneer Mormon Women," *Western Humanities Review* 9 (Spring 1955):145-64; Thomas C. Romney, "Representative Women of the Church: Annie Wells Cannon," *Instructor* 85 (February 1950):42-43; Andrew Jenson, "Annie Wells Cannon," in *LDS Biographical Encyclopedia* 3:334-36; Annie Wells Cannon, "An Intimate Sketch of Home Life," *Relief Society Magazine* 3 (Feb. 1916):66-71; Patricia Rasmussen Eaton-Gadsby and Judith Rasmussen Dushku, "Emmeline Blanche Woodward Wells: 'I Have Risen Triumphant,' " in Burgess-Olson, *Sister Saints*, pp. 459-78; and typescripts and manuscripts by and about Annie Wells (Cannon) generously supplied by her granddaughter, Dr. Phyllis Southwick, Bountiful, Utah. These include Margaret Cannon Clayton, "Our Mother," nineteen-page typescript; Annie Wells's story of her courtship and marriage; Amy Brown Lyman, "Mrs. Annie Wells Cannon," typescript of a tribute given by Sister Lyman in 1934 when Annie Wells Cannon was given a medal and honored as an outstanding woman in civic service.

Chapter 17. *Mary E. Woolley Chamberlain: Handmaiden of the Lord, An Autobiography* (Salt Lake City [?]: Published by the family, 1981).

Index